CENTERBEAM

CENTERBEAM

Edited by Otto Piene and Elizabeth Goldring
Introduction by Lawrence Alloway

Center for Advanced Visual Studies
Massachusetts Institute of Technology

© 1980 by The Massachusetts Institute of Technology

All rights reserved. No part of this book may be
reproduced in any form or by any means, electronic or
mechanical, including photocopying, recording, or by
any information storage and retrieval system, without
permission in writing by the publisher.

Printed and bound by Spaulding Company, Inc. in the
United States of America.

Sponsored in part by The Council for the Arts, M.I.T.

Distributed by The MIT Press
Library of Congress catalog card number 80-68325
ISBN 0-262-66047-4 (paper)

Typesetting and design by Rahman Typographics,
Cambridge, Massachusetts.

Table of Contents

Introduction	Lawrence Alloway	5
Contributions		7
Preface	Jerome B. Wiesner	9
Recognition (In Praise of Centerbeam)	Otto Piene	10
Massachusetts Institute of Technology Center for Advanced Visual Studies	Otto Piene	13
Acknowledgements	Otto Piene Elizabeth Goldring	16
"Centerbeam"	Otto Piene	20
"Centerbeam"	Lowry Burgess	26
An Aqueduct to the 21st Century	Manfred Schneckenburger	27
Ein Aquädukt ins 21. Jahrhundert	Manfred Schneckenburger	30
Gyorgy Kepes		36
"Centerbeam"—Kassel	Elizabeth Goldring	37
"Centerbeam"—D.C.	Elizabeth Goldring	45
Poem On	Mark Mendel	52
"Centerbeam"—Description and Plan for *documenta 6*, 1977	Elizabeth Goldring	54
Steam	Joan Brigham	69
Neon-Argon Line	Alejandro Sina	71
Laser and Music/Sound Lines	Paul Earls	72
"Centerbeam" *documenta 6*—"Centerbeam" Washington, D.C.	Harriet Casdin-Silver	77
Solar Tracking of Holograms for "Centerbeam"	Walter H.G. Lewin Stephen Benton Jim Ballintine Patricia Downey Kenneth Kantor Michael Naimark Brian Raila	79
The Sky Events—Piene's Flying Sculptures	Elizabeth Goldring	82
Technology for Art	Otto Piene	87
Fellows, C.A.V.S.		93
Past Fellows		94
"Centerbeam" Artists, *documenta 6* "Centerbeam" Artists, Washington D.C.		96
Vienna Biennale		97
Biographies		98
Concluding Remarks	Elizabeth Goldring	125

Lawrence Alloway   **Introduction**

"Centerbeam" was a combinative work. The title referred both to its organizing principle and to the M.I.T. Center for Advanced Visual Studies of which the artists were all Fellows. Its creators neither put existing works together nor fused their styles; each artist made him or herself responsible for a characteristic part of the structure. The elements were artist-coded. The whole work was a sum negotiated by the artists in the interest of unity. Otto Piene suggests that the acts of collaboration can be regarded as the content of the work: "Centerbeam is a metaphor of the community of volunteers forming daily symbioses (the relationships of a democratic society)". Thus the creative act, so often described in terms of introspection and arcane procedure, is socialized in group activity. This does not always occur in collaboration; it depends on working conditions that include prior consultation and a structure that requires the coordination of intricate parts. The conditions of joint creativity and the finding of a shareable ensemble, as well as the details of a complex work of art, are the subjects of this book by the participants.

The successful interaction of the artists may have been helped by the fact that the collaboration was a once-only affair, a special occasion, though this is not always sufficient to make things work. For example, at "9 Evenings: Theatre and Engineering" in New York, 1966, the artists retained their traditional autonomy while trying to work socially, resulting in a pile-up of uncoordinated schedules, dissolving responsibilities, and conflict-ing dominations. "Centerbeam", although layered with different contributions, was unified by a belief that collaboration is one of the things that an artist should be able to do and do well. As the product of a group, "Centerbeam" implicitly resisted the twentieth century cultivation of individuality and the creation of works of art as its expression. However, individuality was not sacrificed. This was not a workshop with a master and apprentices or assistants, but a collaboration of equals in which the artists' requirements of personal control were preserved within the group enterprise. A crucial point was the discovery of a containing principle in which they could work freely without disrupting an overall unity. As is recorded in the pieces that follow, it was Lowry Burgess' proposal of "a very long bundle of pipe-lines of elements and energies" that gave "Center-beam" its form, "a root system turned on its side" (Elizabeth Goldring). The ensemble was like a path-node diagram, a graph of processes: its 144-foot length insisted on the directional path, but the nodes opened up into subsystems. There were islands of special functions, transmissions of light, sound, and steam outside the structure itself, and zones of spectator participation in the form of manual controls of the steam and lights.[1]

The coherence of the containing system was remarkable. As well as incorporating a varied set of objects, it was a highly legible configuration. A work of this scale needs a resonant visual image, architectural with symbolic potential, such as a triumphal arch, a maze, or a baldacchino. The form of "Centerbeam" is cyclopean, both in its vast size and in the sense that it monumentalizes a one-eyed vanishing point perspective. Viewed from the ends, it appeared to rush toward the horizon. Viewed from the sides it was an amalgam of aqueduct (a term used several times in this book), pipeline, and wall. The perspective line radiated energy in the forms of light, sound, and steam, reaching out in the plane of the spectators and also rising above to signal its presence as lights materialized in the indeterminate shapes of steam.

The metal and glass structure had two aspects, according to the time it was viewed. Its diurnal-nocturnal cycle gave the structure an extraordinary image of inflection. It possessed a kind of Renaissance aspect by day, an extended corridor displaying a rational and systematic form: hard-edged, reflective, processional. In its schematic clarity and inventive wit it was perhaps analogous to the perspectives of streets designed by Sebastiano Serlio for the theatre (mixed archi-tectural styles for comedy; classical for tragedy). By night its function as a source of energy was stressed by the maximized play of lasers, neon and holograms. The prismatic reflections of the day were not inert, but at night the sense of volatile energy was enhanced. Evocations of space technology replaced the daytime association with the greenhouse, though even this was tinged by the suggestion of hydroponics in the trough of vegetation. At night "Centerbeam" glowed, pulsed and radiated: the energies of transmission were given visual form. On twenty-five nights it was accompanied by sky events, large, helium-lifted sculptures in floral and stellar shapes, and on the last two nights by performances of *Icarus,* a sky opera.[2]

Art critics commonly use a perpetual present tense to discuss works of art, but since "Centerbeam" no longer exists, the past tense seems appropriate. It was, as many large works and some collaborative ones are, temporary, or, as Reyner Banham has put it more roughly, expendable. Since the perma-nence of art is often identified with the uniqueness of the artist, the production of temporary art opposes conventional absolutist aesthetics. In fact, temporary art has a long history, including occasional architecture and ceremonial sculpture; it is art geared to specific events: in time, not timeless. "Centerbeam" could presum-ably be assembled again, but at present its record consists of two appearances, one in Germany and one in the United States.

"Centerbeam's" two locations were very different.

The first installation was in the grounds of an extensive park as part of an international art exhibition, *documenta 6,* at Kassel in Germany. Here it was seen by two tiers of spectators, the art audience that traveled to Kassel and the resident population. We can say that it was seen by both a preselected and a general audience, one trained in art and one responsive to the sense of occasion, of something going on, generated by the enormous show. The second installation, on the Mall in Washington, D.C., dispensed with the initiated audience and functioned as a fully public work. There is no doubt as to the work's popularity, its power to attract attention, and its durability, a necessary requirement of art in unprotected sites. The high level of public interest was not simply the result of the opportunities for spectator participation built into "Centerbeam". The scale of the great shaft, the visual effect of high technology, and the festival aspect of the changing lights and sounds, engaged and held the attention of viewers. This is a prime requirement of public art in spaces of unspecialized function, unlike art in a museum or gallery, where the audience goes expressly to see works on display.

By comparison, the press was reserved about "Centerbeam", perhaps in part because most art criticism is keyed to extolling the creative act in terms of its privacy and singleness. It is no accident that the best known public artist is probably Christo, who stresses individualism in his work. A contributory reason may have been the Center's affiliation with M.I.T. and its government, specifically defense, funding sources. If so, this is ironic, for it is a fact that without institutional sponsorship, whether academic, corporate, or governmental, few public projects in art would be realized today. "Centerbeam" required support at a government level in two countries.

As opportunities continue to arise for the realization of large-scale work, the importance of "Centerbeam" will emerge. Neither the social occasions nor the technical means available to artists are likely to change in the foreseeable future. Hence the singular value of the documents collected in this book. At one point Paul Earls remarked of "Centerbeam" that "backstage is onstage", a phrase that applies to the descriptions collected here. This is typified in the collaboration of Harriet Casdin-Silver with the scientists and engineers who devised the solar tracking system for her holograms. In her written statement and in others this book enables us to share the working out of a complex sculpture, to see the artists defining their own skills and preoccupations while allowing for affiliation and compatibility. But more than that, these documents are a handbook for group work and a model for future collaborations.

[1] Another aspect of the interface of spectator and "Centerbeam", video screens showing the spectators intercut with pretaped material, was unsuccessful because of maintenance difficulties.

[2] These activities represented a climax of the Zero Group's Night Exhibitions, begun in the late 1950's. See *Zero,* edited by Otto Piene and Heinz Mack (Cambridge, Massachusetts; M.I.T. Press, 1973; originally published in Germany, 1958-1961).

Contributions

"Centerbeam" *documenta 6*

Alcoa Foundation
Corning Glass Works Foundation
Documenta GmbH
International Telephone and Telegraph Company
Laser Creations, Inc.
Lubing Maschinenfabrik
Massachusetts Institute of Technology
Spraying Systems, Inc.
Thyssen Henschel
United States Embassy, Bonn, Germany
United States Information Agency

"Centerbeam" D.C.

American Speaker Company
Aries Music Company
Coherent Radiation
Comsat
The Computer Factory, Inc.
Corning Glass Works Foundation
Crown International
Electro-Voice
Carpenter Division of Gardner Cryogenics
General Electric Company
Goddard Space Center
Government Service Administration
Indofex, Inc.
Toshiro Itakura
Massachusetts Institute of Technology
Milwaukee Art Center
National Endowment for the Arts
National Park Service, National Capital Region
Phillips Petroleum Company
Pittsburgh Plate Glass
Smithsonian Institution
Spraying Systems Company
Steam Rent, Inc.
Sylvania GTE
Tapco, Inc.

7

Preface

The Center for Advanced Visual Studies at the Massachusetts Institute of Technology was created twelve years ago, in the fall of 1967, after a completed conversion of M.I.T. Building W-11, 40 Massachusetts Avenue, into artists' studio, office and workshop space (architect, Marvin Goody). Formerly less distinct in appearance, the building had served as the M.I.T. Coop, and subsequently, while housing operations of the Boston educational TV station, WGBH, it suffered a fire. Gyorgy Kepes, the founder and first director (until 1974), enjoyed, together with the Center's first Fellows, a dedication ceremony in March, 1968, which shared initiation rites with the Center for Theoretical Physics.

Twelve years of work at C.A.V.S. have passed with a changing configuration of artists, and with more artists currently working at the Center than ever before. Extensive educational activities have augmented the Fellows' personal endeavors.

The Center is participating in a new interdisciplinary M.S. program which admits M.S. students who intend to become environmental and media artists. The purposes of C.A.V.S. have remained the same since its inception: collaboration of artists with artists and collaboration of artists with scientists and engineers.

The listing of participants in the C.A.V.S. group piece, "Centerbeam", identifies fourteen artists, five scientists, and five engineers. We have to add to the list a number of students both in the arts and in science and engineering. In the process which hatched "Centerbeam" an important concern became manifest: integrated efforts are necessary to create works of art which affect complex contemporary issues and address a sociologically complex audience. Likewise, the artists' work reverberates in the scientists' and engineers' thinking and development.

"Centerbeam" addresses itself to values not commonly considered content in works of art—energy and technologically transported communication. The 144-foot-long composite performing sculpture is a group work attracting large numbers of people in public situations, at *documenta 6* in Kassel, Germany, or on the Washington, D.C. Mall between the National Capitol and the National Air and Space Museum. New artistic media, such as laser projections, holography and flying sculpture—which find themselves serving large audiences via their technically implemented scale—are essential to the piece.

Artistic, poetic expression of energy and message-carrying media requires familiarity and sympathy

Jerome B. Wiesner
President
Massachusetts Institute of
Technology
Cambridge, Massachusetts
photograph: Karsh, Ottawa

with the technical elements of these media and their expressive potential. The integrated neighborhood of artists, scientists and engineers at M.I.T. breeds awareness of new possibilities and promotes the desire to explore new artistic territory. We gladly shared our venture with an international as well as immense national audience by presenting "Centerbeam" at *documenta 6* and in Washington (in cooperation with the Smithsonian Institution and the National Park Service, National Capital Region). I am confident that visitors to these "Centerbeam" installations were moved to understand that M.I.T. is a place where new ideas meet new means, thus inspiring new art of an environmental scale.

Jerome B. Wiesner, President
Massachusetts Institute of Technology

Recognition
In Praise of "Centerbeam"

To relegate "Centerbeam" temporarily to paper does it justice vis-a-vis its nomenclature as a "temporary sculpture". While its hard parts—as opposed to its vital organs, such as the laser — are mothballed in a warehouse, the whole "beast" is asleep like Snow White — to be awakened or not. Even if no new opportunity will blow it into shape again — "Centerbeam" and "Centerbeam" D.C. enjoyed good lives in Kassel and Washington. Documentation in this brochure is a case of Hegel's "Aufhebung" — cancellation, storing, and elevation in one act — which adds to the states of aggregate through which the "bundle of energies and media" (Burgess) keeps passing.

It started with my determination (as in the Group Zero days, twenty years ago) to make a group environment, an animated material expression of spirit, minds and hands of the Center artists and their matches among scientists and engineers at M.I.T. Manfred Schneckenburger of *documenta 6* provided the occasion; Jerome Wiesner, president of M.I.T., and Walter Rosenblith, provost of M.I.T., added encouragement — *in re* and *in spiritu.* In the ensuing peacefully competitive search among C.A.V.S. artists for an encompassing idea, Lowry Burgess' concept: "Centerbeam", gathered following and artistic momentum fast and most vitally. A kinetic, performing energy and media group sculpture was born which has no immediate precedent known to me, in art and literature, music, theatre, opera and celebration. It became a matter of awe, enthusiasm, and exuberance, and a *pièce de résistance* which engendered puzzlement, indifference and intellectualism. Some reviews praised it as a kind of Jesus-of-the-laser, and some spat on it as if a new railroad devil was pushing forward on the tracks.

Popular acceptance was almost instant — with children horsing about the water prism during the days in Kassel or D.C., and with crowds gathering around the laser-and-steam play night after night. Artists from all over paid most serious homage to object and display with colleagueal loyalty. Public media — newspapers, radio, television — greeted the group effort, the art and technology interaction, and the open-air display with fair attention (sometimes dutifully dramatizing the un-drama of our basically lyrical effort). While the galleries' and dealers' art world and their gazettes stood by in opaque silence we demonstrated — I think — a rare case of agreement between artists, government and a broad, public audience. It must be acknowledged that in Kassel and Washington our main sponsors, besides M.I.T., were public agencies, both German and American. On the National Mall in D.C. three major U.S. government branches made "Center-

beam" possible: The Smithsonian Institution, the National Park Service, and the National Endowment for the Arts. Corporate support was invaluable. My 23 sky events and the two evenings of "Icarus" by Paul Earls and me comprising a total of 25 sky events on the Mall were made possible largely by a generous gift of helium from Phillips Petroleum and its subsidiaries. I walk about with a peculiar but — I presume— understandable private satisfaction (and general pride in the success of "Centerbeam"): Despite the extensive use of technology and despite active, engaged and joyful public participation in "Centerbeam" and the sky events, no ankle was sprained during nights and days of inspired communication between the artists and an audience measuring 300,000 by conservative estimates and 1,000,000 by optimistic estimates. A case for public art was made again. Its performance may be gentler and less competitive than sports or disaster and war games. Its effects may be subtler and less obvious — but it does maintain a peaceful way and preclude physical harm. Proper dosage requirements apply to the highly exposed situations of "Centerbeam" as they do in a most private studio, home, or school.

My love and respect go to all artists participating in our "Centerbeam" venture, and my admiration and thanks to the engineers and scientists who invested their skills and enthusiasm. I feel like saying a prayer of thanks for fair weather in Kassel '77 and good weather in Washington in the summer of '78, and I thank, more specifically, Elizabeth Goldring for her work and loyalty to "Centerbeam" and to Center causes.

Another major project, the "Sky Art Conference", will likely occupy us for the next two or three years. It will endeavor an artistic perspective similar to "Centerbeam": to heave artistic expression into the 21st century.

Otto Piene
Gordes, 20 August, 1979

"Centerbeam" on the
National Mall
Washington, D.C.
summer, 1978
by 22 artists with science
and engineering advisors
Center for Advanced Visual
Studies, M.I.T.
"Milwaukee Anemone"
(Otto Piene)
photograph:
Elizabeth Goldring

Otto Piene

Massachusetts Institute of Technology
Center for Advanced Visual Studies

The Center for Advanced Visual Studies at M.I.T. offers a unique situation where artists—currently fifteen resident and twelve non-resident Fellows—develop their work in association with the artistic and scientific community at M.I.T. They are particularly encouraged to use the vast technological, scientific and engineering resources and laboratories available at the Institute. During its twelve years of existence significant work in areas such as laser, holography, video, kinetic and environmental art has originated from the Center's 40 Massachusetts Avenue building in Cambridge.

C.A.V.S. was founded by Gyorgy Kepes as a workshop and forum for outstanding artists. When I became director in 1974, I set forth the following priorities for the Center: 1) environmental art and design on a large scale, to enhance the physical and psychological environment; 2) developmental media work, to expand the influence and accessibility of art for the audience at large; 3) interaction of art and technology, to master the increased scale of communication; 4) the art of celebration; 5) education toward the new arts and general education toward a broader environmental understanding. The past few years have seen a greatly expanded teaching commitment at C.A.V.S., including our participation in a new, interdisciplinary M.S. graduate program (Master of Science in Visual Studies).

The primary role of the Center for Advanced Visual Studies remains to inspire and make possible exceptional artistic work. Its group exhibitions have included "Explorations", at M.I.T.'s Hayden Gallery and the Washington D.C. National Collection of Fine Arts, Smithsonian Institution, which concerned itself with new avenues of interactive and environmental art; "Boston Celebrations", commissioned by Boston's Institute of Contemporary Art in 1975, which was an exhibition of proposals for temporary visual celebrations at specific sites in the city; a second exhibition at the Institute of Contemporary Art in 1976, "You Are Here", which presented proposals by various Fellows of the Center for environmental art on Boston's historic Long Wharf. In the fall of 1975, C.A.V.S. organized "Arttransition", a major international conference, series of events, and exhibition of contemporary efforts to expand art beyond traditional practice, via technology.

The two appearances of "Centerbeam" at *documenta 6* and "Centerbeam" D.C. in 1977 and 1978, respectively, are the main subjects of this publication, along with C.A.V.S. participation in the '79 Vienna Biennale for Graphics and the Visual Arts.

Center for Advanced
Visual Studies,
Building W-11
Massachusetts Institute of
Technology
40 Massachusetts Avenue
Cambridge, Massachusetts
02139
photograph:
Nishan Bichajian
C.A.V.S./M.I.T.

1. Brian Raila
2. Ken Kantor
3. Werner Ahrens
4. Joan Brigham
5. Mark Chow
6. Derith Glover
7. Astrid Hiemer
8. Mira Cantor
9. Mike Moser
10. Mike Naimark
11. Alejandro Sina
12. Elizabeth Goldring
13. Lowry Burgess
14. Paul Earls
15. Gyorgy Kepes
16. Otto Piene
17. Harriet Casdin-Silver

"Centerbeam" participants
Center for Advanced Visual
Studies, M.I.T.
Cambridge, Massachusetts
1977
photograph:
Nishan Bichajian
C.A.V.S./M.I.T.

Acknowledgements

The appearances of "Centerbeam" in 1977 at *documenta 6,* Kassel, Germany, and in 1978 on the National Mall in Washington, D.C., were made possible through the enthusiastic support and donation of time, services and materials by many individuals, institutions, and corporations. The initial momentum was sustained and enforced by guidance and support of M.I.T.'s president, Dr. Jerome B. Wiesner, and provost, Prof. Walter A. Rosenblith, who offered continuing personal encouragement and M.I.T.'s endorsement in each instance.

The *documenta 6* showing was partly funded by Documenta GmbH under the stewardship of Manfred Schneckenburger. Another major sponsor of the Kassel venture was the United States Information Agency whose belief in our work is much appreciated. Other sponsors included the Alcoa Foundation, Corning Glass Works Foundation (special thanks to Robert Ivers), International Telephone and Telegraph Company, Laser Creations, Inc., Lubing Maschinenfabrik, Spraying Systems, Inc. and Thyssen Henschel.

While preparing "Centerbeam" for *documenta 6* we were concurrently negotiating its future appearance in the United States with the National Endowment for the Arts (Visual Arts and Museum Programs) and museum directors. Initial encouragement and impetus to exhibit "Centerbeam" in this country came from Leon Arkus, Director of the Museum of Art, Carnegie Institute; Joshua Taylor, Director of the National Collection of Fine Arts, Smithsonian Institution; Abram Lerner, Director of the Hirshhorn Museum; Carter Brown, Director of the National Gallery; and Charles Blitzer, Assistant Secretary for History and Art at the Smithsonian. Blitzer put us in touch with Mary Ann Tighe, then of the Federal Council on the Arts and the Humanities of Joan Mondale's Art Commission. Her enthusiasm and decisive action in finding an appropriate location in Washington sparked the U.S. action.

Our collaboration with the Smithsonian Institution and the National Park Service, National Capital Region, to produce the "Centerbeam" D.C. involved many offices and officers to whom we are indebted.

Susan Hamilton in Charles Blitzer's office became our liaison with the Smithsonian Institution. Her understanding of what we wanted to do and her personal desire to let it happen helped to set our course and continued to be invaluable. We relied substantially on the guidance of Michael Collins, then Director of the National Air and Space Museum and Melvin Zisfein, James Dean and Jack Whitelaw of NASM. Their continuing affirmation and warmth eventually led to NASM as our most tangible hospice and shipping address. The inspired advocacy and personal commitment of Janet Solinger, Director of the Smithsonian Resident Associates, generated much catalytic energy. Her office commissioned the "Centerbeam" poster and lithograph and organized, through the efforts of Edward Gallagher, lectures by Otto Piene, Paul Earls, and Harriet Casdin-Silver. Other individuals at the Smithsonian to whom we owe thanks for responsive efforts are Robert Burke, Director of Protection Services; Al Rosenfeld, News Bureau Chief; James Mahoney and Maureen Healey in design services; James Symington, Director of the Office of Membership and Development; and Larry Taylor, Coordinator of Public Information.

Our liaison in Manus Fish's office at the National Park Service, National Capital Region, was Joseph Ronsisvalle, with whom we worked out the location, siting and permissions for installation. We are especially grateful to him and the NPS/NCR staff for their guidance throughout and for the careful advice and concerted efforts of Gordon Sulcer, Superintendent of the National Park Service, National Capital Region, prior to and during the installation.

Washington government agencies who offered expedient, enthusiastic, and necessary endorsements and cooperation include the National Fine Arts Commission (reinforced by Charles Atherton's personal encouragement); the D.C. Architectural Commission; the Federal Aviation Administration; the Secret Service; and the Bureau of Radiological Health in the U.S. Department of Health, Education and Welfare. The General Services Administration, with the much appreciated assistance of Jack Galwardy procured our vital workshop space in the navyyard and equipment for installation and performances.

We are grateful for a grant from Comsat Corporation and for a chairman's action grant awarded us by the NEA—especially to Gordon Braithwait, David Searles, Brian O'Doherty and Ira Licht for their understanding support. We also thank Toshiro Itakura for his generous contribution.

Without substantial materials contributions we could not have afforded to produce Centerbeam. Our list of contributors includes: American Speaker Company (sound shuffle equipment); Aries Music Company (sound shuffle equipment); Coherent Radiation (laser equipment); The Computer Factory, Inc. (computer equipment); Corning Glass Works Foundation (glass tubing); Crown International; Electro-Voice (speakers); General Electric Company (wiring); Goddard Space Center; Indofex (TV monitor); Milwaukee Art Center ("Milwaukee Anemone"); Phillips Petroleum and Gardner Cryogenics Division of

16

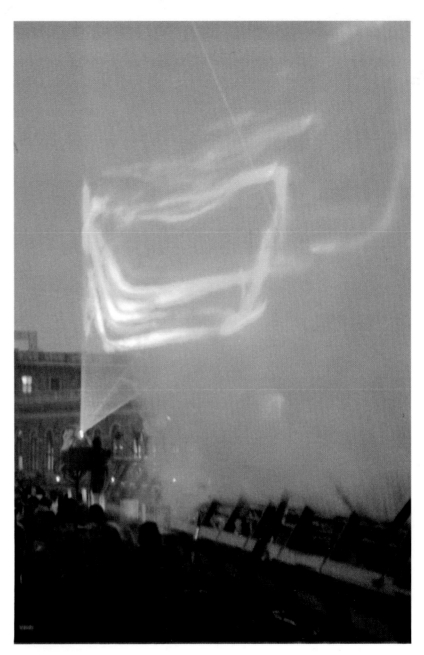

"Centerbeam"
documenta 6
Kassel, Germany, June 24
through October 2, 1977
by 14 artists with science
and engineering advisors
Center for Advanced Visual
Studies, M.I.T.
with "envelope" laser
projection (Paul Earls,
Gyorgy Kepes)
on steam (Joan Brigham)
photograph: Dietmar Loehrl

17

Otto Piene
Director, C.A.V.S./M.I.T.
at *documenta 6* in Kassel,
Germany, summer, 1977
photograph: Mira Cantor

Carpenter Technology Corporation (helium for 25 sky events); Pittsburgh Plate Glass (water prism glass); Spraying Systems Company, Inc. (nozzles); Steam Rent, Inc. (steam generator); Sylvania GTE (lighting, and special thanks to George Clark); and Tapco, Inc. (sound shuffle equipment).

Finally, heartfelt thanks to C.A.V.S. artists, friends and staff for the dauntless energy, devotion, and inspiration that it took to realize a group project of this magnitude—especially to Lowry Burgess who contributed the initial idea and artistic concept formulation for "Centerbeam". We would also like to thank Astrid Hiemer for her careful attention to many administrative details, and Charles Patrick for his public relations work in Washington, D.C.

And, to the many returning spectator participants who said they liked it, thank you.

Otto Piene,
Director, C.A.V.S., M.I.T.
Director and participating artist, "Centerbeam".

Elizabeth Goldring,
Fellow, C.A.V.S., M.I.T.
Coordinator, "Centerbeam".

Otto Piene

"Centerbeam"

The Center for Advanced Visual Studies is essentially a workshop for artists employing sophisticated ideas and techniques. As a member of the Massachusetts Institute of Technology community, it offers affiliation with other M.I.T. minds and facilities and encourages mutual inspiration of artists and scientists. Center artists have been invited to be Fellows partly because of their inclination to work in groups: groups of artists; groups of artists, scientists and engineers; groups of teachers and students. The affinity to group work is not due to lack of individuality or to the herding instinct but represents an understanding of the complexities of present-day life: artistic images may still be one man's or one woman's business, but their processing may involve technological expertise even if technology is regarded by some artists as nothing more than an expanding distribution system. It is commonly assumed that art significantly influences the quality of life. The artist's role, then, is to inject art into "life", i.e., the living's doings and environments. Given the magnitude of the living "masses", the scale of art practice and the distribution of art require group efforts and social technologies: the video artist can neither make nor run the broadcasting system; the celebration artist does not walk in a one-woman parade; the sky artist works with physicists, balloon manufacturers and the Federal Aviation Administration to make an artificial rainbow possible, beautiful and safe.

Looking away from the coterie of artists-for-art-for-art-world associations, socially sensitive artists are rediscovering that not only are the heightened moments of life's joy or drama humanly interesting, but everyday phenomena and concerns deserve artistic attention and interpretative activity. To me, energy transfer via art has been a most fascinating miracle ever since I painted "Frequencies" and "Fields of Light" twenty, or so, years ago. Looking at them recently, I remembered a sentence of Bruno Liebrucks, a philosopher whose classes I took in Cologne in the fifties: "How is it that people do leave a museum or a concert hall *refreshed?*" The regenerative capacity of art quite probably is rooted at a "basic" level of information possibly "below" the level of semantic communication. However, regardless of the level or "value" of energy transfer and "communication" (semantically articulated information), the two dispositions constitute the substance of the artist's work in its effects on people.

Beyond the psychic workings of art, energy transfer and communication have massively apparent social importance in our densely populated world. To appoint them a "theme" of art work simply expresses interest in "what really counts" in "contemporary life". Looking at sets of remotely related pictures reveals the "timelessness" of basic formal languages. The skylines of Munich and Chicago show semblance when confronted, although the "rocketing" buildings of historic Munich are churches and the Chicago high-rises are office buildings. The formal timelessness is being displayed regardless of culture, religion, or era. Yet it is the "eternity" of the shell, without the animal, the timelessness of *formality*. It does not signify identity and individuality — ergo not the full meaning of human expression in private formats or in publicly accessible formats (such as churches, shrines, or office complexes). A church becomes a church because of highly specific symbols encoded in individual, expressive (mostly "artistic") language and the intensity ("energy") with which the symbolism is conveyed depends on the vividness ("quality") of expression— "strong" (beautiful) if "art" is the vehicle and vessel; common, bland, ugly (boring) if profane, utilitarian practice attempts "to do the job".

To consider "Centerbeam" a mere formal arrangement, in sculptural fashion ("minimal", "constructivist", possibly even "op" because of its 144-foot water prism) is as much a misjudgement as to consider a house "a shape". It is the formal organization (yes, that too) of transmitting envelopes for energy and communication media, along with those very media and their offspring, that constitute the whole "Centerbeam" and an entire host of activities and events evolving from it and facilitated by it.

"Centerbeam" is the house qua house and the "Household" comprised by those who live in the house using it as a house: a medium of expression; a place to live, to rest, to entertain guests, to go through generations of human life. Like the house, "Centerbeam" is nothing without its users, inhabitants, human contributors; who are making sense of it, but articulated sense as if "activating" inanimate matter. "Centerbeam" without its artist-creators and audience of participants is an empty shell. However it invites animation because of its supply of energies and media, form come alive, as it "houses" elements: water, air, fire (light) and manifest terrestrial energies: electricity-turned-music; video; light/laser projections; gases (helium to fill flowers to ascend from the earth-based material parallelogram towards the sky, the live-in space of the future).

"Centerbeam" is a metaphor for the community of volunteers forming daily symbioses (the relationships of a democratic society): the gardener (grow-line); the plumber (water line, steam line); the teacher (poetry); food and fork suppliers (brine line, holograms); warming and feeding energies transmitted either via "satellite" metaphors or

"Centerbeam"
Washington, D.C.
programmed steam
emissions (Joan Brigham)
photograph:
Calvin Campbell/M.I.T.

as laser performance. The helium flowers promote transformation of optical energy into "spiritual" energy (via "beauty" again—e.g., water prism).

On special occasions, frequently at night, people and things around "Centerbeam" start dancing. The evening performances with laser projections on the hissing, billowing steam screens and on helium-inflated, floating volumes of polyethylene make the herd of sensual phenomena coalesce and side with nature's generously supplied contributions: wind to shape and move steam clouds and the flower; a sky with stars or rain as backdrop and wrapping foil; leaves and clinging dew to catch projections and refract light. The community of artists, viewers, art work, technology and nature together celebrate moments of rare harmony. The phenomena speak strongly; sound borders on noise; laser light is on the fringe of searing; wind gusts into steam so that ghosts of vapor hover, pirouette and vanish; the steam operator, immersed in wet clouds, appears to be a new Flying Dutchman or Captain Ahab.

Into this exuberant, friendly inferno, the laser projections emerge with distinctly identifiable imagery: moving, changing mouths, eyes, ears, stars, flowers, letters in and on layers of steam, on trees and inflated floating forms of flowers, stars and humans convening to form a recognizable flying polis of pictures. They whirl about in this human/natural mini-universe of a scale ("Centerbeam" is 144 feet long[1]) which permits many people to endorse the images but avoids "Big Brother" proportions of Orwell's nightmare.

The largest images occasionally emitting from "Centerbeam" are the flowers: up to 250 feet long, made of soft, gas-filled envelopes of polyethylene and fabrics. Following the weather, they bob and sway gently or tear diagonally in vivid dialogue with the wind. Due to the price of helium, the flowers appear only at posted dates like fireworks, car races or Easter masses.

The multimedia performances of computerized laser projections are clearly temporary, conditioned by ambient light levels. From the start, "Centerbeam" has been intended as a temporary, adaptable installation of a kinetic, performing, participatory sculpture. Viewer participation includes the manipulation of holograms (solar-tracking mirrors); the obvious play with human images and objects transposed into spectral hues and rainbow shapes through the water prism; the computer-encoding of laser space drawings by audience participants;[2] the "video reflections"; the launching of flowers and other features which require understanding, interference, and initiative of visitor/viewer/participants.

The argument that "Centerbeam" is not "sculpture" or "art" because it does not last is "classroom intellectualism". Permanance in sculpture is only a share of relative impermanence. I remember fondly Jean Tinguely's militant "Be static—only movement lasts". The moonwalk, admittedly, was several degrees more gigantic than the benign "Centerbeam", and the modest "Centerbeam" dangers (such as hot steam and laser light) do not measure up to the risks of space flight. The essential difference, however, is that the moon patrol was sheer spectator sport for those who were not there, i.e., everybody but the three champions. "Centerbeam" is touch-me-feel-me sculpture and the opposite of the fully air-conditioned museum or spectator sport situation. (Even knowing what not to touch becomes part of knowing how to play "Centerbeam" as a toy of energy and poetry for today's children.)

Permanence (or impermanence if you wish) has been newly interpreted since photography. The passing event can be documented in still pictures, on film and audio and video tape. The temporary moon walk is hardly less permanent than the Mona Lisa, with all the media eyes that have passed it onto stores of retrievable images. More obviously than heretofore, reality comes in layers, and the thinner wads are sandwiches of celluloid. How "real" reality becomes appears to be a question of distribution—at least, where "public reality" is concerned. "Centerbeam" occupies poetic territory, a land of promise where private and public reality meet—where private spheres get absorbed by the gulping appetite of the public domain. With all the written and printed reports, slides, video tape, media coverage and the Richard Leacock/Jon Rubin "Centerbeam" film, our "temporary sculpture" will be more reliably "factuated" than Columbus' discovery of *what?*

It is close to being superfluous and redundant to say that "Centerbeam" is a sculptural and performance system rather than a fan of forms in a fixed aggregate state. It is a facilitating device as well as a mannequin come alive with changing dresses—and it is also form for optimal reception of sunlight—becoming a potential energy-generating sculptural system as well as poetic demonstrator for the workings and intertwinement of energy "rays" and manipulated, pre-refined earth energies.

The flexibility and adaptability of the display-and-performance system make it possible for "Centerbeam" to change location. Moving from Kassel to Washington, D.C., "Centerbeam" changes appearance and performance almost to the point of changing its identity as it migrates to another social, geographic, ecological, political, financial

situation—and attempts to make available for
artists and audience the most literate means of
expressing basic forces of contemporary life. To
draw our experiences into the realm of general
literacy via sensual vehicles follows the worthiest
traditions in art.

The pleasant and entertaining naiveté of "Centerbeam"—along with its sophistication, ambition and
multimedial convincing power—is the basic naiveté
of art: the attempt to capture the universe in a
nutshell. Our nutshell is 144 feet long; it projects
sensory apparatus (mouths and eyes) onto—and
sometimes impersonates—a cloud.

"Centerbeam" is an artist model for collaboration
among artists, scientists and engineers who, working together, energize and sensitize fellow minds
in a given environment. Sharing experiences, i.e.,
intensified, sublime communication among many,
is the intention; this time, it is taking the form,
language and complex expression of "Centerbeam".

[1] In Kassel; in Washington, D.C., 128 feet.
[2] In the "Centerbeam" installation in Washington, D.C..

Lowry Burgess
concept drawing for
"Centerbeam"
documenta 6

Lowry Burgess
concept drawing for
"Centerbeam", D.C.

Lowry Burgess   **"Centerbeam"**

On a raw overcast Saturday in December three years ago about 10 of the Fellows at the Center gathered in the alley beside the Center to set up the first small test of the elements of "Centerbeam". We had collected from all our studios an assemblage of what were to become some of the major elements of "Centerbeam": some clouds of wind-blown steam, a three-foot glass water prism, pulsing neon rods, a small argon laser and scanners, a hologram, a TV and other miscellaneous pieces. These were gathered in an impromptu changing collage. At first the alley was empty but within fifteen minutes more than eighty people stood in the cold watching the pulsing, flowing, steaming sketch. During those moments we all knew that "Centerbeam" could be what we had thought. In the next two years many people would be enthralled, perplexed, and delighted by the work.

During the past 12 years, the Fellows of C.A.V.S. have used diverse substances and technologies to form works of art. Congruent with our scientific and technological involvement has been a shared desire to extend the parameters of art. We have collaborated with other artists, scientists and engineers to shape works which live more freely in both the physical and social environment. "Centerbeam" for *documenta 6* has been conceived, executed and installed in this spirit. "Centerbeam" emerged from Otto Piene's attempt to define a project commensurate with these directions which would involve the work of many artist/Fellows at the Center.

I proposed a work in which a very long bundle of pipelines of elements and energies were incrusted with numerous images and informational elements (video, holograms, laser, antennae, mirrors, etc.) This woven bundle was to be absolutely straight and level running through the landscape and possibly some buildings. It appeared to me as a living staff of energies, media, and phenomena like sparkling notations.

I hoped that we would see the integration of all our efforts into a coherent union—a single, strict, yet highly elaborated form—thereby creating an intensity and symbiosis beyond any specific technology, media or context. What appealed to me was the occasion to work with both human and environmental relationships not readily available in our individual work. In all this process it has been both remarkable and rewarding that such a diversity of minds and hearts can find a nesting structure.

"Centerbeam" produces constant palpitations which irritate every facet of the structure, weaving substantial, phenomenal and energetic threads. Although it is large, it registers human gestures and

responses. Seen closely, it is an aggregate of small, delicate parts. As a bundle of lines it is a consensus about axis and relationships. A set of parallel lines in the landscape creates a territory, a domain, separating and articulating a "here" and "there", a "this" and "that".

Metaphorically, "Centerbeam" is a moment as full of portent as Petrarch's:

One day, hunting—I used to hunt—
I opened trees enough to find her,
Glancing sun, wild naked, stretched in cold
       water . . .
I am sparked flame, I am the ugly bird whose
       huge wings raise her.

(Petrarch23. Nel dolce tempo de la prima etade. Translation: N. Kilmer)

"Centerbeam" is a glimpse into a new place, into a new freedom, soul and potentiality:

. . . when the wild river valley and the woods were bathed in so pure and bright a light as would have waked the dead . . .

Even ice begins with delicate crystal leaves, as if it had flowed into moulds which the fronds of water plants have impressed on the watery mirror.

. . . but in the morning the streams will start again into a myriad of others . . . As the sun gets higher, the most fluid portion, in its effort to obey the law to which the most inert also yields, separates from the latter and forms itself a meandering channel or artery within that in which is seen a little silvery stream glancing like lightning from one stage to another . . . .

In the silicious matter which the water deposits is perhaps the bony system and in the still finer solid and organic matter the fleshy fibre or cellular tissue . . . .

Who knows what the human body would expand and flow out to under a more congenial heaven? What Champollion will decipher this hieroglyphic for us, that we may turn over a new leaf at last?

(Henry David Thoreau—*Walden*—Spring)

"Centerbeam"
documenta 6
during installation
(laser try-out)
photograph: Dietmar Loehrl

Manfred
Schneckenburger

An Aqueduct to the 21st Century

1

The incongruity was premeditated. A *documenta*
with the expressed objective of doing equal justice
to technically conditioned media was the result of
three generations of images which had been
technically processed via photography, film, video.
The main focus was on new off-shoots of repro-
ducible art, while new art worlds emerging from
the resources of technology applied to environmental expansion were represented — almost — only
by "Centerbeam". "Centerbeam" was the only
"art machine": a multi-media kinetic dragon in
which technology did not purport to reproduce
worlds of images, but created its own action
theatre of environmental steam explosions,
prismatic reflections, multi-colored neon-bands,
laser lines. "Centerbeam" certainly was not an
extraneous element (on the contrary!), but it was
an exception.

Does the lonely appearance of this aqueduct of
elemental forces and energies reflect an abatement
of the far-reaching art and technology movement,
culminating at its peak in 1970, with the famous
exhibition in the Los Angeles County Museum?
Does it represent a withdrawal from the technical

joy of avant-garde experimentation which is
expressed in the parallel archaic, regressive tend-
encies of a few "track-safe" or "subjective
archeologists"? Have we at least in Europe, while
following a trend of the Seventies, become more
skeptical of an art which exists under the auspices
of technology? It took a long time before the
technological aspect of photography was not
viewed as an argument against its artistic potential.
Today, after the utopia-conscious ferment of the
Twenties and the Sixties, are we in the process of
transferring our old mistrust of a technical art
dependence onto the new, non-reproducing media
of environmental art?

The question can be addressed, even self-critically,
to numerous critics who saw "Centerbeam" less as
a polemic and more as a popular display zone in
the *documenta* spectrum. But the antitechnologi-
cal sentiments discussed again and again since
William Morris — the idea that "machines" are
incommensurable with art — is an outworn argument in the context of 20th-century art history.
The machine-fascination of the constructivists and
suprematists, Duchamp and Dada, has led the
cliché of the mésalliance of art and technology ad
absurdum. Technological premises have been
combined — see the example of *Zero* — with an

27

almost romantic relationship to nature, wind, water, growth. The wide resonance of "Centerbeam" with its audience (which defeated the perplexed, helpless silence of a few critics) shows the dimension of emerging possibilities. Projects like "Centerbeam" are not aiming at the technical standardization of our imaginative faculties but seek rather to open new areas of visual fantasy and participation. I do not believe that the polemic "art and technology" discussion has to be conducted again.

2

The fields of tension vis à vis art/technology reach back far enough for historical reference. There is a remote kinship between "Centerbeam" and the steaming, hissing, flashing stage machines of Baroque theater and the almost forgotten air art of fireworks, which was an integral part of the Baroque total work of art. A more direct line can be drawn to the machine art from the heroic early phases of modernism: Tatlin's "Memorial to the 3rd International", El Lissitsky's electromechanical picture stage, Moholy-Nagy's "Manifesto of the dynamic-constructive power system" (published in 1922) and accompanying light apparatus, the ironic alienation of the Duchamp and Dada machines. In 1928 constructivists and Dadaists celebrated a "festival of technology" in Hanover, for which Schwitters wrote an opera. The spirit of technology speaks: "Sparks! Lightning! Fire! Light! Machines! Machines! Iron. . ." In 1930 Moholy-Nagy built the fundamental incunabulum of kinetic, environmental light art with his light-space modulator (light and movement being the principal ingredients of kinetic art into the Sixties).

Those who put stock in historical precedent can even build a direct bridge from Moholy-Nagy's light machine to "Centerbeam". Moholy-Nagy arrived in the U.S. in 1937 to assume the directorship of the New Bauhaus in Chicago. In the same year he called his countryman Gyorgy Kepes to the school. In 1946 Kepes became a professor at the Massachusetts Institute of Technology. In 1967 he founded the Center for Advanced Visual Studies whose directorship Otto Piene assumed in 1974. A long-standing European tradition of experimental art and technology was united with American technologies of the Sixties and Seventies, and all this after American art was entirely carried by the action painting myth of total artistic subjectivity a decade earlier. "Centerbeam" has grown out of cooperation among artists, scientists and technicians, in keeping with one of the working modes at the Center. Collaboration in a collective which assigns to each artist a clearly defined realm has found an almost ideal working model in "Centerbeam".

Antecedents can also be found on the technological side. The history of art in the 20th century among other things is a history of the discovery and independence of new media, be they elemental appearances of nature or new-found, invented forms of energy. Several of the media presented by "Centerbeam" previously belonged to the repertoire of a technologically experimental art. A few names stand for many more: Thomas Wilfred, Moholy-Nagy, Nicolas Schoeffer, Heinz Mack, Hans Haacke, Gyula Kosice, etc. Otto Piene expanded their vocabulary to include light, air, fire, water. Already in 1964, the London Center of Advanced Creative Studies proclaimed not only light and movement but also "heat, sound, optical illusion, magnetism, contraction and expansion of substances, water, the movement of wind and foam, fire, smoke, and numerous other natural and technological appearances" as its materials. In 1968 Willoughby Sharp could organize an air art exhibition in Philadelphia which included steam, smoke and helium. Barely on the market, laser beams have been employed since 1962 for ever more perfect light drawing by C.F. Reutersward and then by Robert Whitman, James Turrel, the Japanese Uematsu, and, partly in cooperation with the Center, by Rockne Krebs. In 1968 Finch College Museum in New York presented the first, however dilettantishly modest, exhibition of holograms. Video, since its first artistic use by Nam June Paik in 1965, already has had its own history within the framework of present-day art. "Centerbeam", despite its special position, can therefore offer a number of previous experiences as part of its artistic strategy.

3

Nevertheless, "Centerbeam" distinguishes itself quite basically from all previous or simultaneous attempts. "Centerbeam" draws a kind of encyclopaedic sum from about twenty elementary powers and energies which are orchestrated into an impressive performance of sensations and participation. The tally sheet of systematics ranges from biological growth processes to the archaic powers of water and wind, the early industrial basic energy of steam, the many forms of artificial light, the information systems of radio and video, the three-dimensional pictures of holograms and the wiring strategies of electronic complexes. Viewed as such, "Centerbeam" appears as an attractively dramatized, abridged survey of technological advancement since the beginning of the First Industrial Revolution and even further back, as a visualization of energies and impulses as they have shaped the history of human civilization and been translated into artistic media of the 20th and 21st centuries. "Centerbeam" shows these new media —without a doubt—in an "adze state" of transition from the mechanical to the cybernetic age, whose possibilities it projects. The horizons of utopia appear to be wide open—again.

The use of some individual media — by comparison to the highly developed mechanic, electric and electronic excitement of the Sixties — appears almost modest. "Centerbeam" does not use technology to set off superlative fireworks of technological brilliance or — like *Zero* — to sublimate nuances of a highly aesthetic light choreography. The linear functionalism of the aqueduct presents itself rather didactically, although not without kinetic and coloristic moments and the playful participation of its audience. The demonstration of new ways is more important than an opulent avant-garde gesture, the suggestion of utopia more important than its full realization in 1977. Therein lies the unpretentious honesty of "Centerbeam".

At the same time it is obvious that this observation does not do justice to the artistic uniqueness of "Centerbeam". It is evident that without exception the emphasis is on the sensual-visual qualities of elements and energies, and it is these which have been clustered for the program. The degree of total visualization provides a touchstone of their transformation into artistic media. Criticism of the "show" tendency of "Centerbeam" misjudges its specific performance character. The dramaturgy is complex: dramatic show effects (the rhythmic explosion of steam, the linear rippling flow of stroboscopic lamps) change with subtle nuances of perception (changing hologram colors due to observer-position and sun-angle; the time shift of musical sequences) and analytic fascination (the laser-fan). Effects are precisely calculated and augment each other: the colored laser light encounters the diffuse eruptions of steam. The 144-foot water-prism has the effect of a triangular glass prism which glisteningly multiplies the programmatic changes. The video images, as a blend of audience images and pre-produced tape material, overcome the passive attitude of the spectator and enable the "Centerbeam" performance to provide an autogenerative (participatory), changing, reflecting situation.

Translation, Dagmar Kohring

Manfred Schneckenburger

Ein Aquädukt ins 21. Jahrhundert

1.

Das Mißverhältnis war kaum zufällig. Eine documenta mit dem erklärten Ziel, auch technisch konditionierten Medien zu ihrem Recht zu verhelfen, war vor allem durch drei Generationen technischer Reproduzierbarkeit—Fotografie, Film, Video—bestimmt. Der Schwerpunkt lag auf den neuen Zweigen am alten Stamm der abbildenden Kunst, während die Entstehung neuer Kunstwelten aus dem Fundus der Technologie, die environmentale Ausweitung des Kunstbegriffs—fast—nur durch den "Centerbeam" vertreten war. "Centerbeam" blieb die einzige "Kunstmaschine": ein multimedialer kinetischer Drachen, in dem die Technik keine vorgegebenen Bildwelten reproduzierte, sondern ihr eigenes Aktionstheater environmentaler Dampfexplosionen, prismatischer Spiegelungen, verschiedenfarbiger Leuchtbänder und Laserlinien inszenierte. Dazu kam ein ausgeklügeltes Partizipationsprogramm von Radiomitteilungen und Videospiegeln. "Centerbeam" blieb so gewiß kein Fremdkörper (im Gegenteil!), aber er blieb eine Ausnahme.

Spiegelt sich in einer solchen Isolation dieses Aquädukts für Elementarkräfte und Energien ein Abklingen der weiträumigen Art and Technology—Bewegung, die 1970 in der berühmten Ausstellung im Los Angeles County Museum ihren euphorischen Höhe-aber auch Wendepunkt fand? Liegt darin ein Rückzug von der technischen Experimentierlust der Avantgarde, wie er parallel dazu auch in den archaistischen, regressiven Tendenzen einiger "Spurensicherer" oder "subjektiven Archäologen" zum Ausdruck kommt? Sind wir, wenigstens in Europa, einem Trend der siebziger Jahre folgend, skeptischer geworden gegenüber einer Kunst im Zeichen der Technologie? Es hat lange gedauert, ehe der technische Anteil an der Fotografie nicht mehr als Argument gegen ihr künstlerisches Potential betrachtet wurde. Sind wir heute, nach den utopiebewußten Anläufen der zwanziger, der sechziger Jahre dabei, das alte Mißtrauen gegenüber einer technischen Bedingtheit der Kunst einfach an die neuen, nicht-abbildenden Medien der Umweltkunst weiterzugeben?

Die Frage läßt sich, durchaus auch selbstkritisch, an zahlreiche Kritiker richten, für die "Centerbeam" weniger eine polare Grundposition als eine populäre Schauzone im documenta—Spektrum zu besetzen schien. Aber die seit William Morris wieder und wieder diskutierten antitechnologischen Ressentiments, die Idee, "Maschinen" stünden im Widerspruch zur Kunst, sind durch die Geschichte der Kunst im 20. Jahrhundert längst überholt. Die Kunst selber, angefangen bei der Maschinenfaszination von Konstruktivisten und

Suprematisten, von Duchamp und Dada hat das Klischee von der mésalliance zwischen Kunst und Technik ad absurdum geführt. Technologische Voraussetzungen konnten sich—das Beispiel Zero—mit einer garadezu romantischen Einlassung auf Natur, Wind, Wasser, Wachstum verbinden. Die breite Resonanz, auf die "Centerbeam" beim Publikum stieß (und die im Kontrast zum hilflosen Schweigen mancher Kritiker stand) zeigt die Dimension der Chancen, die sich hier auftun. Projekte wie "Centerbeam" zielen nicht auf die technische Standardisierung unserer Vorstellungskraft, sondern öffnen neue Räume visueller Phantasie und Partizipation. Ich glaube nicht, daß die polemische Diskussion "Kunst und Technik" noch einmal geführt werden muß.

2.

Die Kontinuität des Spannungsfeldes Kunst-Technik reicht weit genug zurück für historische Anknüpfungen. Es gibt eine entfernte Verwandtschaft des "Centerbeam" mit den illusionistischen Fertigkeiten dampfender, fauchender, blitzender Bühnenmaschinen des Barocktheaters oder mit der fast vergessenen Himmelskunst (air art) der Feuerwerke, die ein geachteter Teil des barocken Gesamtkunstwerks waren. Auf einer direkteren Linie liegt die Maschinenkunst einiger Künstler aus der heroischen Frühphase der Moderne: Tatlins "Denkmal der 3. Internationale", El Lissitzkys elektromechanische Guckkastenbühne, Moholy-Nagys 1922 veröffentlichtes "Manifest des dynamisch—konstruktiven Kraftsystems" mit den sich anschließenden Lichtapparaten, die ironische Verfremdung der Maschine bei Duchamp und Dada. 1928 feierten Konstruktivisten und Dadaisten in Hannover ein "Fest der Technologie", für das Schwitters eine Oper schrieb. Der Geist der Technologie tritt auf: "Funken! Blitz! Feuer! Licht! Maschinen! Maschinen! Eisen . . ." 1930 baut Moholy-Nagy mit seinem Licht-Raummodulator die fundamentale Inkunabel der kinetischen, environmentalen Lichtkunst, wie überhaupt Licht und Bewegung bis weit in die sechziger Jahre Hauptelemente des kinetischen Entwicklungsstrangs sind.

So kann, wer auf säuberlich verkettete historische Linien Wert legt, sogar eine unmittelbare Brücke von Moholy-Nagys Lichtmaschine zum "Centerbeam" schlagen. 1937 kommt Moholy-Nagy in die U.S.A, um die Leitung des New Bauhaus in Chicago zu übernehmen. Im gleichen Jahr beruft er seinen Landsmann Gyorgy Kepes an die Schule. 1946 wird Kepes Professor am Massachusetts Institute of Technology. 1967 gründet er hier das Center for Advanced Visual Studies, dessen Leitung 1974 Otto Piene übernimmt. Eine europäische Tradition des Kunst und Technik-Experiments vereinigt sich mit amerikanischen Technologien der sechziger und siebziger Jahre, nachdem die

"Centerbeam"
documenta 6
opening night
photograph: Dietmar Loehrl

amerikanische Kunst ein Jahrzehnt zuvor noch ganz vom action painting-Mythos der totalen künstlerischen Subjektivität getragen war. "Centerbeam" wächst aus der Zusammenarbeit von Künstlern, Wissenschaftlern, Technikern, wie sie zum programmatischen Selbstverständnis dieses Instituts gehört. Das Zusammenwirken in einem Kollektiv, das jedem Künstler einen klar definierten Teilbereich zuordnet, hat im "Centerbeam" ein geradezu ideales Arbeitsmodell gefunden.

Anknüpfungen finden sich auch für technologische Details. Die Geschichte der Kunst im 20. Jahrhundert ist—unter anderem—auch eine Geschichte der Entdeckung und Verselbständigung neuer Medien, sei es der elementaren Erscheinungen der Natur oder neu gefundener, erfundener Energieformen. Folgerichtig gehören etliche der Medien, die "Centerbeam" präsentiert, schon vorher zum Repertoire einer technisch experimentierenden Kunst. Wenige Namen stehen für viele: Thomas Wilfred, Moholy-Nagy, Nicolas Schöffer, Heinz Mack, Hans Haacke, Gyula Kosice und, immer wieder, Otto Piene dehnten ihr Vokabular auf Licht, Luft, Feuer, Wasser aus. Das Londoner "Center of Advanced Creative Studies" proklamierte schon 1964 nicht nur Licht und Bewegung, sondern auch "Wärme, Klang, optische Illusion, Magnetismus, Zusammenziehung und Ausdehnung von Stoffen, Wasser, die Bewegung von Wind und Schaum. Feuer, Wind, Rauch und zahlreiche andere natürliche und technologische Erscheinungen" als seine Materialien. 1968 konnte Willoughby Sharp in Philadelphia eine Austellung "air art" organisieren, die Dunst, Rauch, Helium mit einschloß. Laserstrahlen wurden, kaum auf dem Markt, seit 1962 von C.F. Reuterswärd, dann von Robert Whitman, James Turrell, dem Japaner Uematsu oder, in Verbindung mit dem Center, Rockne Krebs immer perfekter als Lichtzeichnung eingesetzt. Im New Yorker Finch College Museum gab es 1968 die erste, wenngleich noch dilettantisch simple Ausstellung von Hologrammen. Video hat, seit seiner ersten künstlerischen Nutzung durch Nam June Paik im Jahr 1965, bereits seine eigene Geschichte im Rahmen der jüngsten Kunst. "Centerbeam" kann so, ungeachtet seiner Sonderstellung, eine Menge vorausgehender Erfahrungen in seine künstlerische Strategie einbringen.

3.

Dennoch unterscheidet "Centerbeam" sich ziemlich grundlegend von allen vorausgehenden oder gleichzeitigen Versuchen. "Centerbeam" zieht eine Art enzyklopädischer summe aus rund zwanzig Elementarkräften und Energien, die zu einer wirkungsvollen Performance aus Sinneseindrücken und Partizipation komponiert werden. Charakteristisch ist die Systematik der Aufzählung, die von biologischen Wachstumsprozessen

über die archaischen Kräfte des Wassers und des Windes, die frühindustrielle Grundenergie Dampf, die verschiedenen Erscheinungsformen künstlichen Lichtes, die Informationssysteme Radio und Video bis zu den 3 D-Bildern der Hologramme und den Relaisschaltungen elektronischer Komplexe reicht. So gesehen, erscheint "Centerbeam" als eine attraktiv dramatisierte Kurzfassung technologischen Fortschritts seit dem Beginn der 1. Industriellen Revolution und weiter zurück, eine Visualisierung der Energien und Impulse, wie sie die Geschichte der menschlichen Zivilisation prägten, übersetzt in künstlerische Medien des 20. und des 21. Jahrhunderts. "Centerbeam" zeigt diese neuen Medien, wer möchte daran zweifeln, in ihrem "Faustkeilstadium" des Übergangs vom mechanischen zum kybernetischen Zeitalter. Der Horizont der Utopie bleibt weit geöffnet.

Dazu gehört, daß der Einsatz einzelner Medien sich gegenüber manchem weitentwickelten mechanischen, elektrischen, elektronischen Spektakel der sechziger Jahre eher bescheiden ausnimmt. "Centerbeam" benützt die Technik nicht, um ein superlativisches Feuerwerk technologischer Bravour abzubrennen oder—wie Zero—die Nuancen einer hochästhetisierten Lichtchoreografie daraus zu sublimieren. Mit dem strikten Leitungsfunktionalismus seines Aquäduktes gibt er sich vergleichsweise didaktisch, wenngleich mit dem Glanz kinetischer und koloristischer Pointen und dem Reiz einer spielerischen Einbeziehung des Publikums. Die Demonstration der neuen Mittel ist wichtiger als ihre opulente Ausdifferenzierung, die Aufblendung der Utopie wichtiger als ihre volle Entfaltung im Jahr 1977. Darin liegt die unprätentiöse Ehrlichkeit des "Centerbeam".

Dabei ist klar, daß dieser Blickwinkel der künstlerischen Eigenart des "Centerbeam" nicht voll gerecht wird. Entscheidend ist, daß es durchweg die sinnlich-sichtbaren Qualitäten der Elemente und Energien sind, die zum Programm gebündelt werden. In der totalen Visualisierung liegt geradezu ein Prüfstein ihrer Umwandlung in künstlerische Medien. Kritik an der "show-Tendenz" des "Centerbeam" verkennt deshalb diesen spezifischen Vorführungscharakter. Die Dramaturgie ist einsichtig: Dramatische Schaueffekte (die rhythmischen Explosionen des Wasserdampfs, der linear abperlende Fluß stroboskopischer Lampen) wechseln mit subtilen Wahrnehmungsnuancen (die durch Betrachterstandort und Sonneneinfall wandelbaren Farben der Hologramme, die Zeitverschiebung der musikalischen Sequenzen) oder analytischer Faszination (der Laser-Fächer). Wirkungen sind exakt kalkuliert und steigern sich gegenseitig: Das kohärente Licht farbiger Laserachsen stößt auf den diffusen Energieausbruch des Wasserdampfs, der Laserstrahl wird im Dampf kristallinisch pulverisiert, ohne seine Kohärenz zu verlieren. Das durchlaufende Wasserprisma wirkt

als Dreieckspiegel für Licht, Laser, Hologramm,
als ständiger Projektionskristall im Kern der Kon-
struktion, der die Wechsel des Programms glitz-
ernd multipliziert. Die Video-Bilder mit ihrer
Vermischung von Besucheraufnahmen und vor-
gefertigtem Bandmaterial überwinden das passive
Verhalten des Betrachters und ermöglichen die
"Centerbeam"-Performance als sich selber hervor-
bringende, sich verändernde, reflektierende
Situation.

Gyorgy Kepes
Director Emeritus
C.A.V.S./M.I.T.
Museum of Science installa-
tion of retrospective
exhibition — "Works in
Review"
Boston, Massachusetts
1973
photograph:
Nishan Bichajian
C.A.V.S./M.I.T.

Gyorgy Kepes

"Centerbeam" '77 coincided with the tenth anniversary of the founding of the Center. Therefore, it may be appropriate that my comments are based on excerpts from my past writings; "Centerbeam" is an idea-collage—a metaphoric statement of ecological and personal interdependencies. It expresses the aspiration to creatively change our environment.

"Today we live in a world that lacks in richness and vitality, because we are embedded in a 'second nature', in a man-shaped environment which could not grow naturally because it was intercepted and twisted by one-sided economic considerations. The appearance of things in our man-made world no longer reveals their nature: images fake forms, forms cheat functions, functions are robbed of their natural sources—the human needs. Urban landscapes, buildings with counterfeit insides and fake outsides, offices and factories, objects for use, the packaging of goods, posters, the advertising in our newspapers, our clothes, our gestures, our physiognomy are without visual integrity. The world which modern man has constructed is without sincerity, without scale, without cleanliness, twisted in space, without light and cowardly in color. It combines a mechanically precise pattern of the details within a formless whole. It is oppressive in its fake monumentality, it is degrading in its petty fawning manner of decorative facelifting. Men living in this false environment and injured emotionally and intellectually by the terrific odds of a chaotic society cannot avoid injury to their sensibilities, the foundation of their creative faculty."

(from a talk at MOMA, *College Art Journal*, 1947, pp. 18-19)

"The first signs that we have begun to develop an art of public forms and corresponding dimensions came indirectly and almost accidentally some years ago as artists began to rescale their work, unconcerned with civic implications, indeed resentful of them. Canvases increased in size, sculptural forms in dynamic expressive power. These forms strained the storage and exhibition capacity of rooms in houses and galleries and halls of museums. In searching for new strength and for a new physical range for their creative vision, many artists could no longer record their conceptions by using nothing but their own two hands and such traditional tools and media as brush, pigment, and paper, and chisel, wood, and stone. In significant number they reached out for the tools, methods, and materials of modern technology. Of necessity they called upon the scientific and engineering competence of the fabricators of their new materials. Art, thus, without loss of personal vision—in point of fact through the expansion of such vision—is fast approaching the environmental scale and by its own inner dynamics as a craft

becoming a collaborative enterprise involving science and engineering.

"In daring to aspire to explosive goals, artists can discern in the new surroundings spearheads of the imagination: explosive new images as well as the explosive new tools and materials with which to achieve them. In our expanding scientific-industrial urbanized world, however, no man, no matter how imaginative, can possess the whole sweep of creative power needed to reach such goals concretely, that is to say, in full scope and complete detail. A collective vision is needed, the vector, as it were, of the creative impulses of artists, city planners, scientists, and engineers, all working together."

"A similar collective vision born of pooled feelings, ideas, and knowledge is needed to realize another large-scale, potential form for which a demand is becoming open and urgent: mass play activity or choreographed expressive outlet. Men who live riveted to the television set or encapsulated in an office or automated factory have forgotten the joys of shared, happy action. A new pageantry is long overdue, a new collective, cooperative public focus through which the individual can sense the riches of his world more directly. We have prototypes, for example, of mass events in which the participants' uniquely felt kinesthetic experience is interwoven with shared surprise or joy in seeing and hearing themselves simultaneously in amplified dimensions on some audio-video display device.

"The most convincing artistic forms of our time are inner models of structural vitality and social relevance. They give us confidence that in spite of everything there is still richness in life. We can put them to important use, first in the reshaping of the man-made environment in accordance with our best physiological and psychological interest, and, second, in the shaping of our inner world so that our sensibilities and our outer world harmonize."

(from the introduction to the dedication catalogue of C.A.V.S., by Gyorgy Kepes, 1967)

Elizabeth Goldring   "Centerbeam" — Kassel

It is unusual for contemporary artists used to doing their own work to forge a collaborative effort which is not an anonymous statement and at the same time not a clothesline of individual pieces. "Centerbeam" became the integrated expression of 14 artists aided by scientific and engineering consultants. Mature and young artists working together produced a group project composed of identifiable individual contributions. The continuing drama associated with accommodation and adaptation of parts and people, the technical complexity of the project and the difficulties attached to doing the piece in Germany for the *documenta 6* audience made it a rare artistic endeavor leading to a finished piece that was essentially what we had promised.

The process — intense, relatively happy and informative — produced a safe, responsive structure of newness, mobility and adaptability, and it generated enough enthusiasm so that the work moved on to the Washington, D.C. National Mall in 1978. The process is recorded here from notes and observations dating from October, 1976 to August, 1977.

Manfred Schneckenburger, director of *documenta 6,* had spoken with C.A.V.S. director, Otto Piene, about inviting a Center group work to *documenta 6.* As the Fellows worked on various proposals for the exhibition, three concepts emerged: Harel Kedem, a graduate student, suggested a habitat fabricated of abandoned computer-age hardware and software. C.A.V.S. director Otto Piene suggested a diamond structure poised in the landscape which would use various materials and media to amplify the sun's reflected energy. Lowry Burgess, a long-time Fellow of the Center, proposed bundled energy and communications lines from the well springs of an urban environment to extend into the natural landscape, where they would become visible interactive transmissions.

The Fellows reacted favorably to Burgess' proposal, as did Schneckenburger. But after the first generation of renderings and written descriptions, the proposal which Burgess had parented was still a vague "Gare St. Lazare" and metaphoric "aqueduct"; horizontal "Doric column"; "fugue". Then a small group consisting of Piene, Burgess and Michio Ihara began work on the structural design and solidified the concept.

A primal feature of the work was the 144-foot-long water prism. It was originally conceived by Burgess as a trough to be dug into the ground. In the course of our meetings it was determined to be above ground and optically potent. On his return from a trip to Norway, Carl Nesjar suggested an appropriate design for the stanchions of an elevated prism. Debate ensued about the relation-

ship of the pipelines to the trough: should they be arrayed in spaghetti fashion over the trough, centered vertically above it, or arranged diagonally to one side? For reasons of safety, the third option was agreed upon.

Piene suggested a "landing strip" or reflective surface to provide a "dancing floor for the light". Ihara proposed building a reflecting pool under the whole work. Piene disagreed, feeling that the whole thing would become too formalist and unapproachable, making the prism itself just a pretty object. A laser was introduced as a strong kinetic/performing element. Paul Earls suggested that it spread in a spectral fan and be used to generate large images on steam screens. It soon became apparent that what we were planning to construct was a 144-foot horizontal "building". Piene pointed out that even at that length the piece was not endless. Consequently, the beginnings and endings of the sculpture were seriously debated as well as whether the work should crescendo or remain repetitive and constant all along the way.

"We should put as much of the activity as possible in the structure itself. We should build a repetitive, predictable work resembling a root system turned on its side." (Burgess)

After much debate we decided to avoid a denouement and that the materials pipetted through the work might be dumped into a small pool at one end. The question of beginnings and endings remained a serious issue.[1]

As vital to us as the sculptural and performing elements of the piece were its participative and didactic connotations. Should supporting information about the piece be transmitted throughout the beam, and, more importantly, to what extent could visitors actually play the work? Ideas ranged from Alejandro Sina's strong, simple suggestion of a speaking tube which would run the length of the work to Paul Earls' elaborate proposal for time-activated systems keyed to pitch and melody. Active "terminals", including viewer-positioned holograms and video images, became part of the sculpture.

Our insistence on participation made us pay attention to security and maintenance problems. It was obvious that much of the equipment was expensive and fragile. There was some thought of building a surveillance system into the piece itself; concern about raising the laser high enough so that it would not be harmful; possibly jacketing the steam line so that it would not be hazardous. The neon and argon tubes had to be encased in some kind of waterproof glass, as did the holograms. Lockable housings had to be provided for some equipment, especially the generators. Mechanical surveillance and maintenance devices were proposed but dis-

Stored putti
documenta Park (Karlsaue)
Kassel, Germany
photograph:
Elizabeth Goldring

Peacock
documenta Park (Karlsaue)
Kassel, Germany
photograph:
Dietmar Lohrl

carded in favor of human presence—one (possibly two) full-time person(s) to guard, service and repair the piece.

Decisions concerned both the aesthetic and practical sides of the sculpture—aluminum, galvanized and gold-plated metals could be interesting but would be more expensive and less durable than steel. Kedem suggested that the sculpture was "too slick and sterile"; that he would like to include more organic materials, such as rope, wood and cloth.

"Let's not be too concerned about nature. After all, *documenta* occurs in the loveliest of baroque parks, so if we are artificial, perhaps it doesn't matter. There will be several New York artists carrying their sods and grasses to Kassel." (Piene)

Conversions—voltages, amperages, and pipe threads—were explored as we tried to determine what to buy in Boston and what to purchase in Germany.

Power consumption became a central issue. We thought about incorporating alternative energy sources. Alejandro Sina suggested that a wind sculpture could power his neon/argon rods. Solar tracking for the holograms would emphasize sun energy. Other suggestions for using alternative energy systems came from M.I.T.'s president, Jerome Wiesner, who proposed that the video tapes render coal movers, mining operations and other energy imagery and that we should look into photosynthesis and photoseparation.[2]

The specific imagery—or poetry—of the parts was largely personal with respect to contributions: Paul Earls' tape of a botched multiband rendition of a Boston 4th of July salute, "Stars and Stripes", conducted by Arthur Fiedler; Gyorgy Kepes' unfolding envelope to be projected via laser on a steam screen.

The video imagery motifs were the most difficult to supply. We did not want to compete with the planned installations of video artists—including those from the Center.[3] There were endless suggestions for natural imagery—clouds, water, Niagara Falls—monitors floating like lily pads in a pool at one end of the sculpture. We finally decided to show Aldo Tambellini's early tapes.[4] The "sounds" were also difficult to resolve and resulted in a session at the end of a long day: laughing parrots, tree pippets' mating songs, the crowing of roosters and much laughter were projected (and later rejected).

The colors of poppies, cornflowers and peacocks would be incorporated. We thought about including a beer line or a drinking fountain. Burgess felt that if people were to drink the water running through the sculpture they would help to keep it clean.

In addition to frequent (two or three per week) group meetings, each member of the group monitored the details of his or her contributions. Joan Brigham, who would produce the steam for "Centerbeam", continually countered suspicions about the visibility, or invisibility, of mid-summer steam. A large, dense cloud was necessary for laser projections. She tested the strength of generators, assembled 200-foot lengths of pipe along a railroad track in Cambridge and tried out fittings. Paul Earls and Joan Brigham conducted laser/steam experiments with a "DREAMSTAGE" laser from Earls' exhibit at Carpenter Center, Harvard University.

Alejandro Sina's neon/argon samples glowed in our meeting room. Harriet Casdin-Silver and students, together with physicist Walter Lewin, sandwiched daylight holograms and developed the solar tracking system. The holograms became a vital part of the piece, but some of us were concerned that "Centerbeam" should not be a necklace for holograms. The brine line was tested in the freezing lab at M.I.T., and Walter Lewin computer-plotted the projected spectral effects that the water prism would display at predictable sun angles.

A small-scale glass water prism was set up in the alley adjacent to C.A.V.S. and complemented with neon, argon, laser and steam lines. In the "pit", the C.A.V.S. communal studio space, we produced a full-scale mock-up of several "Centerbeam" sections on which we rehearsed for Nishan Bichajian's photographs for the *documenta 6* catalogue. Those photographs came to resemble the "real thing", indeed.

Where was the money to come from? Certainly not from the Center's modest operating budget. A fund-raising strategy had to be developed and implemented. Otto Piene and I assembled a large portfolio of written and visual descriptions which we carried to New York and Pittsburgh corporations and Washington, D.C. endowments and other government organizations. The proposal received enthusiastic responses—much better than we had anticipated—but it was clear that potential financiers were less willing to support an exhibition in Germany than an installation which would become highly visible in this country. We decided that it would be worthwhile to plan future "Centerbeam" exhibitions at various U.S. locations—in Washington, D.C, Pittsburgh, New York, Boston and other places (the Fellows' suggestions included the midwestern prairies and deserts of the southwest). An early conversation with Joshua Taylor, Director of the National Collection of Fine Arts, Smithsonian Institution, led to discussions with David Scott and Carter Brown of the National Gallery, Abram Lerner and Steve Weil of the Hirshhorn Museum, and Charles Blitzer, Assistant Secretary of the Smithsonian Institution.[5] This meant that we

Lowry Burgess (left)
Nam June Paik (right)
at *documenta* site
summer, 1977
photograph: Dietmar Loehrl

must design a "moveable feast" — a structure we could disassemble and reassemble — which we eventually fabricated in 8-foot modular sections.

M.I.T.'s president, Dr. Wiesner, became a strong advocate of "Centerbeam" and personally secured Aloca's and International Telephone and Telegraph's support for the project. The United States Information Agency supported the work enthusiastically and contributed substantially to the funding of "Centerbeam" as well as encouraging a catalogue and film about the piece.

In addition to our fund-raising activities, Piene made several trips to Kassel to negotiate money, materials, accommodations and siting with Manfred Schneckenburger. From a map of the *documenta* grounds, we had determined two potential locations for the piece — a "stepped site" and a "field site". The "stepped site" turned out to be a war memorial so the "field site" prevailed. We conjured details of the site scanning aerial views of the *documenta* grounds with a magnifying glass and looking at Otto Piene's March photographs. By early May, however, it was still unclear how we were going to do it "there" and precisely where "there" was.

When Burgess, Bill Cadogan and Werner Ahrens arrived in Kassel, roughly a month prior to the *documenta* opening, good working relations were established with the *documenta* bureau which included their allocation of an adjacent garden shed (indispensable to the construction phase of "Centerbeam") and communal living quarters for our group on Frankfurter Strasse (again indispensable: ensuing early morning breakfast meetings helped to formulate and structure communal activities).

By the second week in June most of the artists had come to Frankfurter Strasse and were engaged in preparing their contributions for "Centerbeam" as well as working on the piece as a whole. The artists arrived to find the stanchions in place and peacock blue after the birds which occasionally wandered about the park. The first flowing water inside the prism glass turned "Centerbeam" into an optics performance. The arrival of the steam generator which was impressively craned into place cast the piece as a "steam engine". The holographic protrusions of forks were more vivid, refined and spectacular than we had imagined — and popular from the moment they were attached. When the laser arrived, there were inevitable safety

Otto Piene
at *documenta* site
during construction of
"Centerbeam"
June, 1977
photograph: Mira Cantor

Construction of
"Centerbeam"
documenta 6
(laser housing)
photograph: Mira Cantor

problems. However, the laser-scanned image projections turned on for the first time at opening night worked magically.

Late afternoon on the day before the opening Piene let his 50-foot red flower unfinger itself in the green grass near the sculpture. The air-inflated flower lifted by polyethylene helium-inflated loops rose silently and spectacularly into night ground-fog and mist, lighted by a full moon and ground lights. After a few hours he let it fly away. It went up redly as we watched it travelling off into the night sky.

"Centerbeam" was huffing and puffing exactly an hour before the opening and launched its first nighttime performance: the unfolding and folding envelope and star images of laser light on moving clouds of steam. The performances were repeated nightly throughout the duration of the exhibition. The piece had strong daytime appeal, too, which invited visitor play with the water prism and holograms.

By the third day of *documenta 6* many exhibits had been vandalized, but "Centerbeam" for the 100-day duration remained intact (perhaps because people were afraid of "the beast"—and because they liked it). During the week prior to de-installation filmmakers Jon Rubin and Richard Leacock arrived in Kassel with Burgess, Piene and Earls to produce a film on "Centerbeam". As a part of our "closing ceremonies", Piene flew a second "Kassel flower" in miserable weather.

[1] Artistically "unresolved" to date.
[2] Coincidentally, the emergence of "Centerbeam" collided with revitalized energy concern in the U.S. and the appointment of Dr. Schlesinger as Energy Secretary. It fostered interest on the part of the Smithsonian Institution and the Vice-President's Committee on the Arts in exhibiting the piece in Washington, D.C.
[3] Peter Campus, Antonio Muntadas, Douglas Davis, and Ron Hays.
[4] Ca. 1968.
[5] Suggested future sites for Washington, D.C., installations included the crescent adjacent to the White House, the tidal basin area and a site on the Mall next to the National Air and Space Museum, which was to become the site of the 1978 "Centerbeam" installation.

Otto Piene
"Flower"
helium-lifted, air-inflated
sculpture
for "Centerbeam"
documenta 6
Kassel, Germany
summer, 1977
photograph: Dietmar Loehrl

Otto Piene
"Flower"
for the opening of
"Centerbeam"
documenta 6
Kassel, Germany
June 23, 1977
photograph: Alejandro Sina

"Centerbeam", D.C.
photograph:
Calvin Campbell/M.I.T.

Elizabeth Goldring

"Centerbeam" — D.C.

The National Mall land is under the jurisdiction of the National Park Service, National Capital Region, and the national museums lining the Mall are operated by the Smithsonian Institution. These two government agencies—Park and Smithsonian—became the official sponsors of "Centerbeam" D.C. with whom we (primarily Otto Piene and I) negotiated for over a year. The site we agreed upon for the "Centerbeam" installation is the remaining "empty plot" on the Mall slated to become the National Museum of Man.[1]

The physical boundaries of this site are Third and Fourth Streets and Jefferson Drive and Constitution Avenue. Its closest neighbors are the imposing granite, glass and concrete edifices of the National Air and Space Museum; the offices of the Department of Health, Education and Welfare; the "glass house" botanical clymatron; the National Capitol; and, across the way, the East Wing of the National Gallery of Art. By law the

sacred vista or central axis of the Mall from the obelisk commemorating George Washington to the glistening teeth of the Nation's Capitol must remain visually unblocked by either temporary or permanent installations.

To do a project on the Mall means reckoning with the architectural scale which in turn reflects the importance of national treasures, codices and policies and houses the bureaucracies which maintain and feed them and exhibit them to the national and international public.

"Centerbeam" D.C. was not the same version we had exhibited at *documenta 6*. It was more ambitious; local conditions required specific adaptations; and the Kassel experience inspired new directions/dimensions in imagery, performance, and visitor participation.

Kassel had served as testing ground and laboratory for artistic and technical developments and refinements, especially concerning laser projections and steam screens. Piene's sky flowers appearing only

"Centerbeam", D.C.
photograph:
Calvin Campbell/M.I.T.

twice at Kassel became a major focus of the evening performances in Washington. There were 23 sky events in the course of the summer and two premier performances of the sky opera "Icarus" on September 8 and 9. We invited new artists to join our group effort—Paul Matisse, creator of the "Kalliroscopic White River", and Christopher Janney, creator of the "soundshuffle" light walk. The sky events and Matisse's and Janney's contributions brought direct and spontaneous visitor participation. We also omitted certain features such as the brine line (because of cost and Nesjar's conflicting commitment in Norway).

Outdoor laser projections and 250-foot sky flowers are adventuresome projects for any community and need to be carefully pre-registered.[2] Although we worked primarily through Parks and Smithsonian, we had to apply for direct approval of some other federal and local agencies. The D.C. Fine Arts Commission must stamp the forehead of any public installation on the Mall. They heartily endorsed our project but stipulated that directional sound be aimed away from the National Gallery's new East Wing (which opened in the same month as "Centerbeam"). We had to obtain both FAA[3] and Secret Service clearance, which we received expediently and even enthusiastically.

We agreed to notify them before each sky event and keep them informed about unpredictable developments; we promised not to fly sky flowers or "tethered balloons" in winds stronger than 10 knots and to maintain a fixed laser trajectory at all times. (We had hoped to project laser imagery onto clouds and moving screens and had to abandon the idea.)

For practical and ideological reasons we worked closely with Michael Collins, Melvin Zisfein, Jack Whitelaw and James Dean of the National Air and Space Museum. The museum's north wall served as our laser projection screen. (NASM also provided storage facilities, messenger service, a mailing address, bathroom and shower facilities.) We discussed at length and over many months the logistics of flying Piene's flowers and Rainbow[4] from the museum's roof; we all liked the idea, but in the end it was vetoed by the Smithsonian legal office because they were afraid we would fall off the roof or damage it (the roof had only a 3-foot high retaining wall and was surfaced in a fragile material, likely to develop leaks if stepped upon).[5]

Within the Smithsonian Institution, the Office of History and Art, represented by Susan Hamilton, served as our liaison and advisor. Janet Solinger,

"Centerbeam", D.C.
photograph:
Calvin Campbell/M.I.T.

head of the Smithsonian Resident Associates, became an ardent supporter, mediator, and energizer. The Smithsonian Associates organized lectures by C.A.V.S. artists (Piene, Casdin-Silver, and Earls) and commissioned Piene's "Centerbeam" poster.

Once we had satisfied the Park's environmental concerns (primarily whether the laser would kill trees in the vicinity), Representative of Operations Joseph Ronsisvalle and Superintendent Gordon Sulcer in particular helped us with technical issues related to siting and implementation. Parks furnished woodchips for landscaping and installed a protective snowfence prior to installation.

We sometimes had the impression that although we carried a respectable portfolio, Kassel documentation, precise technical specifications—and despite our persistence and serious negotiations—everybody but us considered our project to be an interesting but unlikely exercise. When Parks and Smithsonian finally realized that we were on the brink of actually delivering what we said we would, security, maintenance and publicity became the issues of the hour—necessary operations involving substantial money and personnel commitment. Each of us thought that the other two institutions

ought to foot the bill. In the end the solutions were compromises involving all three parties. We were given an office in a turret of the Arts and Industries building, public relations services, desk, telephone, and a broken IBM typewriter that attempted to spell good morning in Bs, Ts, and Ls. Parks and Smithsonian worked out a surveillance system on the half hour which was complemented by our students' 24 hour guard duty. It is remarkable that in the final analysis, no part of "Centerbeam" was damaged or stolen, given crime statistics in that corridor of the city.

The most difficult last-minute negotiations involved laser protocol for which we were pioneering regulations. The day after the opening, an ominous story appeared in *The Washington Post* about a laser show which was shut down by the Bureau of Radiological Health, Food and Drug Administration, Department of Health, Education and Welfare. The same day Secretary Califano sent a delegation from HEW across the street to check on our laser operations and determine their safety. The ensuing tests on three occasions between the hours of 10 pm and 2 am involved measuring the scattering of the laser beam in steam and required that we provide additional safety labels, kill switches and a walkie-talkie patrol. Despite

47

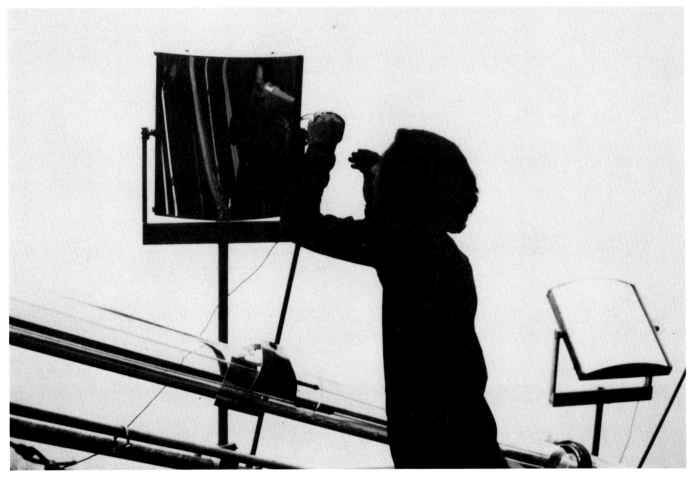

"Centerbeam", D.C.
detail of solar mirror
installation
photograph:
Elizabeth Goldring

these adaptations and much paperwork, they and we moved fast to adopt compliance measures and we received clearance to proceed within five days (a process which could have taken months).

Funding negotiations had been as complicated and time-consuming as the negotiations for permissions of installing "Centerbeam". For a long time the project was in danger of being filibustered for lack of cash for materials and services. M.I.T.'s commitment, a chairman's action grant from the National Endowment for the Arts, a contribution from COMSAT, substantial materials contributions amounting to about $85,000, General Services Administration support which included workshop space, and funds and in-kind services from the Smithsonian Institution and Parks finally made "Centerbeam" D.C. possible. However, the lack of cash forced many of the artists to personally contribute substantially to the project as well.

The two week installation period, roughly from June 5 to 20, 1978, was not without dramatic moments to test the patience of Lowry Burgess, the "Centerbeam" artistic director. The site utilities map (dated 1923) had mismarked a water main so that after two days of futile digging, a hose had to be run from the corner fire hydrant, which sustained us through the summer. "Center-

beam" was sited so as not to interfere with the popular, casual volleyball fields on the lot. The periscoped laser was aligned prudently not to transcend the edges of the northeast wall of the National Air and Space Museum outwardly. The "Centerbeam" structure ("sculpture") was more refined than at Kassel but the steam generator housed in a Steam Rent trailer provided "real-world" counterpoint. Underneath the trailer was the guard's hammock and hibachi. The air-conditioned control hut for monitoring computers, lasers and sound equipment was the only cool place during days of 102°F temperatures. The snow fence initially surrounding "Centerbeam" was rolled smaller and smaller as we and the piece gained confidence vis-à-vis an ever-present audience.

Art students from the University of Maryland volunteered to help with the installation and became an invaluable part of our technical main-tenance and guard force. On June 22, all of the C.A.V.S. artists had "hung their ornaments" and attended an opening reception hosted by the Washington area M.I.T. Alumni Club at the Smith-sonian Institution "castle" after which Otto Piene gave an introductory lecture about "Centerbeam" at the Museum of Natural History to a packed auditorium.

Throughout the summer, the work crescendoed, gathering popular momentum and artistic inspiration. We intentionally began somewhat cautiously or low-key to try out "the beast" on new terrain. In a windless night sky, after trying laser inspection tests, Piene flew his first sky flower[6] at 2 am on June 23/24, 1978. It was "a perfect night" seen by only a few—unlike the 22 ensuing sky events and the sky opera, "Icarus", which attracted crowds of thousands.

The site which had seemed impregnable became truly inspiring. It demanded continuing artistic energies and artistic presence to nurture it—to fly flowers, bring new holograms, draw new laser images, and envigorate each evening laser/steam performance. We had designed a truly collaborative and participatory object/practice. The strength of each performance depended on who was running the steam, operating the laser, flying the inflatables—in order to make it "a good night for environmental art".[7] We suspended performances only twice in 80 days for technical difficulties and only occasionally because of inclement weather.

"Centerbeam's" location on the Mall was quite different from the art exhibition setting at *documenta 6*, and the visiting populations were different too. The omnipresent question "What is it?" forced us to talk a lot and offer several generations of hand-out descriptions. People came in families with blankets and picnics to watch "a show"— sedentary viewing gradually was replaced by active audience participation, especially during the sky events. "Star Wars", "Close Encounters of the Third Kind" and "media symphonies" had precipitated fascination with laser technology, and "How does it work?" was another question often asked. Enthusiasm for "Centerbeam" gradually replaced curiosity. People seemed inclined to enjoy the work more once they learned it was "just art", and we began to see familiar faces interspersed among the crowd of tourists from Maine, Idaho and Japan.

The sky opera "Icarus" comprised our last two evening performances. "Centerbeam" became a stage set/machinery and "Minotaur".[8] The helium-lifted Daedalus singing and playing a violin and the red inflatable Icarus flying sculpture with 150 polyethylene cones for wings (built in our navy yard workshop) joined the Princeton Columbia Boys Choir, flautist Nora Post and the Alexander's Feast musical group in interpreting Paul Earls' music and Piene's ideas of sky theater. The performance was a finale and at the same time a rehearsal for future sky opera performances.

From the start we delivered what we had promised, and finally after September 9 we dismantled

"Centerbeam". We left the site as we had found it, trusting to have made a statement for future impact on public art in Washington. We feel we were able to accomplish "Centerbeam" on the National Mall because of persistence inspired by technological and artistic confidence gained at Kassel and in many other different places before energetic Washingtonians joined us to see "Centerbeam" happen.

[1] See "Centerbeam" — Kassel, pp. 37-40.
[2] Identified precedents in D.C.: Rockne Krebs' 4th of July laser event using the George Washington Monument; hot air balloons on the Mall; Piene's "Washington Sky Ballet" on the Mall in 1970.
[3] Federal Aviation Agency.
[4] Another sky event project.
[5] I like to imagine Piene's large inflatables flying from the whole string of Smithsonian Museums' roofs synchronously.
[6] The "Brockton Flower".
[7] Repeated exclamation and "award" by Marc Palumbo (Maryland student).
[8] Paul Earls.

"Centerbeam", D.C.
with laser projections
(Paul Earls) on steam
(Joan Brigham)
photograph: Walter Oates/
Washington Star

Mark Mendel

POEM ON

RAW FABRIC
CATHODE RAYON DRAPES
VIDEO SYNC AND NAVAHO BLANKET

FLUID HYDRAULIC LANGUAGE
BEAMS
THE BLUE DEN OF JETS

SNOW MELTS ON THE SIZZLING WEAVE
CHILDHOOD
UNCAPTIONED

TELEPOETIC CLOTH
FRICTIONLESS TIME VENT
ICONIC RAY

WHAT SNOW FELL
HERE
THIS FACE RECALLS

ANODE DIODE ELECTRODE NIGHT
NECKLACE STREET SPLIT LIGHT
DIAMOND TAXIES ON ICE

BALLAD ON SONIC GANTRY
OUR CONNECTION
POURED LIGHT

COLOR SLIDES LIGHT TRAILS
MAN TRACKS FLIMSY LINES
TOY SUNS COSTUME VECTORS

STONE BURNS BARE CRUST
RUNNING SHADOW RUNNING EYE
LAVA FLOWERS CLEAR TIME

MEMBRANE FILMS SOLAR GLORY
PHOTOSYNTHESIS PLANET AND STAR
STEPCHILD REFLECTED BEAUTY PLAYED

DIESEL DECELERATION
THE WAVE BEGINS IN THE CHEST
PULLS AWAY IN ALL DIRECTIONS

THIS DANCE A PART OF YOU
DISTANCE APART FROM YOU
BREATH TAKING SHAPES OVER MOONLIT MESA

PAYLOADER TRACKS IN SAND
INDUSTRIAL HEXAGRAM POINTING AWAY
DIRECTIONS FOLLOW DIRECTIONS

COIL WIRE BLUE SPARK
EMBEDDED ROCKET
EARTHBALL FIRED IN THE STAR POCKET

ALL THE VERBS REWIRED MILES
WORDS TO SCAN LIKE LIVING DIALS
EVERY METER FLUCTUATES
THOUGH CONSTANT WITHIN THE DIODE'S GAZE
SOFT FLARE BYRON'S TENDER RAYS

WHEN IT RAINS OUTSIDE IT POURS
OUR LOVE IN A CLOUD OF DOORS
NEON STOCKING ROLL IN STEAM
ICE BLUE ANGEL DREAM

YOUR ART YOUR NATURE
MY SALT IN YOUR SHAKER

GLASS RAY

FROST

WHITE GLAZE

GLASS RAYS

RAY CHARLES

PLAYS

"still

in peaceful dreams

I see

the road

leads back

to you . . ."

RAY

RAY

HAND SWOOPS

OVER FLASHING CONSOLE

CLOUD

UNFOCUSED

AS THE FISH

MANOS

OJOS

MIRRORS

TODOS

MIRRORS MANOS

TODOS

RADIANCE

RADIANCE

RADIANCE

DUST AND RAINDANCE

RADIANCE

RADIANCE

ELEMENTS

IN SELF-EVIDENT LIGHT

APOLLO GLOVE TOUCH

UNDERSEA TOUCH

TOUCH

MAKES THE THERE THERE

THERE

THE AIR THERE

TURBULENT SILVER

LIGHTSOURCE

MOVING ROUGE

DR. J'S JUMPSHOT

SOFT GROOVE

FAINT RAINBOW GROOVE

SOFT ROUGE

PERFUME GREEN

AMARILLO ON ICE

BREATHING STEAM

BLUE SPAN

EXTRUDING GARDENS

BRONZE WIND

TRANSFLUENT

MESH

Elizabeth Goldring

"Centerbeam" — Description and Plan for
documenta 6, 1977

"Centerbeam" encourages us to respond humanly, creatively, unexpectedly and with a shared sense of wit to the bundle of energy and communication lines that have become our network of existence. Conceptually, "Centerbeam" is an aqueduct joining urban and natural environments. Through various combinations of energy transmission and transformation systems on the one hand and poetry, artistry, and humor on the other, it renders the invisible visible and integrates spectator and spectacle.

It is a 144-foot long straight structure carrying pipelines that envelope compressed air, gas, steam, water, ice, neon, sound, electricity, and communication media. The pipelines parallel a water prism which extends the full length of the beam. The pipelines are supplied by appropriate machinery (generators, a compressor, a 4-watt laser, transformers, etc.). At one end of the structure the strongly vertical element of a wind wheel provides a sculptural energy collector and power source. At the other end a small pond catches water pipetted through cooling systems of the piece. Solar-tracked mirrors and timing devices help to orchestrate the events and displays occurring at various points along the 144-foot expanse.

Phenomena incorporated in and surrounding the work are light (sunlight, reflected light, neon, argon, xenon, laser light), sounds (live, natural, electronic, transmitted, processed), daylight holograms, ice formations, and scanned laser images. Within the larger related activities of steam, water, air and light occur numerous small-scale phenomena of sound and video.

The sculpture becomes participative drama as landscape, weather and people interact with it. One part of the sound system is keyed to respond directly to visitor presence (voice and movement). Individuals can also transmit their images through the aqueduct by means of the video beam. At night the work facilitates an intense performance of sounds and lights. During the day participation on a more intimate scale is encouraged by changing spectral phenomena of the water prism and by holograms and video events.

Water Prism

The water prism is a 144-foot long, 7½-ton mass of water supported approximately 4 feet above the ground. It is an open trough shaped as an equilateral triangle with a 20-inch section. It absorbs, refracts and reflects the nuances of natural and artificial light surrounding "Centerbeam".

"Centerbeam"
documenta 6
detail of 144-foot
water prism
photograph: Dietmar Loehrl

The water prism creates haloes around anything reflected in it and straight horizontal lines appear bent or curved on it as one looks into it.

One scientific consultant to "Centerbeam", Dr. Walter Lewin of M.I.T.'s Center for Space Research, developed a computer program which would determine exact widths, angles and placement of the spectra produced by the water prism. Luckily this program confirmed initial experiments.

Some relevant optical considerations are as follows:

In Kassel the water prism's most effective position relative to the sun would have been due east/west. At *documenta 6* it actually occupied an angle NW to SE of 43°. Concerning the configuration of the prism: the wider the bottom angle of the water prism, the wider but paler the displays of spectra; conversely the narrower the angle, the brighter the display. For "Centerbeam" a narrower angle was chosen for the brighter display and because of structural considerations; the strongest spectral appearance occurs at 10-15° from the horizontal surface of the water.

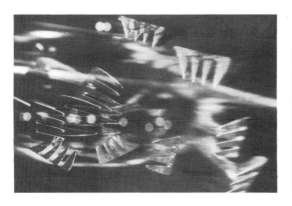

"Centerbeam", D.C.
detail of hologram,
"Equivocal Forks"
(Harriet Casdin-Silver)
photograph: Marc Palumbo

"Centerbeam"
documenta 6
detail of steam jets
(Joan Brigham)
photograph: Dietmar Loehrl

Holography Line

Eight hologram plates, 12½" x 16½", project imagery frontally toward the viewer. They are white light transmission holograms which use the sun or, when necessary, illuminators as their light sources. Holography is the process of recording laser light waves which are then diffracted by the hologram plate or film to reconstruct the 3-dimensional image in space. A hologram is in essence a light sculpture.

Artificial illumination occurs from a white light source (3000°k) behind and above each hologram at a distance of two meters at a 45° angle. The light should have an angular distance of no greater than 1/6° horizontally and 2° vertically. Each holographic image appears in one color at a time, depending on the viewer's angle and the angular position of the light source. The holograms, encased in glass, contain realistic imagery which is projected frontally in space about 3 feet. Extensive visual variation is constituted by movement of the spectator, the artificial light source, or the sun.

Certain holograms are solar-tracked using a servo-controlled system. A 60° arc of a 15-inch-radius cylindrical mirror is mounted on a vertical axis at the required distance and angle from each hologram. Although such mirrors weaken the reflected sunlight, cylindrical mirrors have two important advantages: 1) the curvature of the cylinder eliminates the need to track in the horizontal dimension; and 2) the horizontal angular distance of the sun is required from 1/2° to less than 1/6°. Thus, solar tracking is necessary only in the vertical dimension, permitting the cylindrical mirrors to rock up and down around their horizontal axis. The motion is achieved via a two-directional motor, controlled by a pan of photo cells mounted near the top and bottom edges of each hologram. A logic circuit directs the motor until both photocells sense light and the hologram is illuminated. When there is not sufficient sunlight, power is transferred from the servo system to a halogen cycle quartz spotlamp for each hologram.

Steam Line

The steam system is composed of two independently valved pipes, lines A and B, laid horizontally along "Centerbeam" from the ninth to the eighteenth stanchions.[1] Both lines are supplied from a midpoint located at the fourteenth stanchion, opposite the steam generator, to ensure even distribution of steam flow. The mid-portion of line A is drilled with holes 1 5/8" apart, 5/64" in diameter, in straight sequence extending 32 feet (4 "sections" marked by the equidistanced stanchions). Proceeding from this mid-portion in both directions the straight sequence of holes splits into two lines of holes curving over 16 feet on either side of the pipe and ending at a point 90° from the top. The small holes permit the steam to condense at all exit points, forming a gently spiraling cloud of steam 64 feet long. The height of the plume thus coordinated is subject to the manual operation of the main steam valves. When they are fully open, the cloud extends approximately 30 feet above "Centerbeam".

Line B is composed of a series of individual vertical jets issuing from 3/4" valves. These are placed to form a Fibonaci series, calculated by equating stanchion 19 as 0, stanchion 18 as 1-1, and progressing in intervals of 2', 3', 5', 8', and 16'. The jet at the 1-1 position is fitted with two 2" closed nipples directing their large "bursts" of steam horizontally along the length of the work. The rented Kassel steam generator requires 220 volts producing 1500-2000 kg of steam per hour at 14-16 atmospheres. At maximum pressure combined plumes of steam from lines A and B reach 40 feet in height, thus providing a moving screen for laser projections.

Laser Line: Spectral Fan

A 4-watt mixed-gas (krypton and argon) laser which produces a columnated beam of polarized "white" green light[2] is an essential part of "Centerbeam". It can be directed through a 60° prism so that individual colors of the spectrum become visible. At least ten different colored lines emerge, ranging from bright red to deep blue. The colors fan at approximately 80 inches off the ground. Their journey from the prism to distant trees is made intermittently visible by wisps and clouds of steam.

Laser Line: Projected Images

The laser beams can also be directed onto x-y scanning mirrors mounted on galvanometers whose rotation and position are directed by computer-controlled voltages. Recognizable imagery is projected onto the steam screen. Besides weather conditions—mostly wind—the appearance of the projections is dependent upon the scanning-mirror angles which can be adjusted. At *documenta 6* a micro-computer with digital-to-analog convertors generates the image of an opening and closing envelope as well as images of mouth, eye, ear, flower and several words. Varying geometric star images have been generated on large M.I.T. computers and stored on audio tape. They are decoded on site for transmission to the scanning mirrors and for subsequent projection.

Electricity Line

The electricity line powers the large machinery, i.e., the steam generator, compressors, and laser as well as the sound, video, and hologram-illuminator systems.

Neon-Argon Line

These two lines form the top section of the "Centerbeam" parallelogram of pipes. One red, one blue—they are comprised of glass tubes 1/4" in diameter and 8 feet long, inside a 4-inch diameter, 144-foot-long glass tube. They are filled with neon gas for the red glow and argon/mercury for the blue glow. They are barely visible in daylight but brightly so at night. The gases inside the tubes are energized and timed by a high-frequency power supply. The wind-power generator accommodates consumption of about 50 watts.

"Centerbeam"
documenta 6
laser housing and steam
generator
photographs: Mira Cantor

"Centerbeam"
documenta 6
detail of steam, water and
brine pipes
photograph: Mira Cantor

"Eye"
laser projection
(Paul Earls, Mira Cantor)
photograph: Alva Couch

"Centerbeam"
documenta 6
neon/argon line
(Alejandro Sina)
photograph: Alejandro Sina

"Centerbeam"
documenta 6
detail of laser (spectral fan)
photograph: Mira Cantor

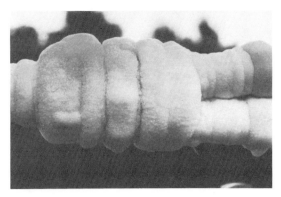  

"Centerbeam"
documenta 6
detail of brine line
(Carl Nesjar)
photograph: Dietmar Loehrl

"Centerbeam"
documenta 6
"dug in" video monitor
photograph: Mira Cantor

"Centerbeam"
documenta 6
video camera installation
photograph: Mira Cantor

Brine Line

The brine line forms a cooling cycle for various parts of "Centerbeam" and specifically creates small ice events within the work. Circular piping of chilled brine is commonly used in refrigeration. "Freon" gas (dichlorodifluoromethane)—maintained at a certain pressure by a compressor—circulates through thin copper coil submerged in a brine[3] container. The freon gas is very cold and, as it circulates in the copper coil, it gradually cools the brine to a temperature lower than the freezing point of fresh water. The chilled brine, when pumped through metal pipe, will cool metal to the temperature, for instance, of -15° (5° F), not only making the surrounding air give up moisture on contact but freezing this moisture to form ice crystals.

Compressed Air Line

The compressed air line extends a jet stream of pressurized air throughout the structure. The compressed air plays with steam, water, and people at specific intervals along the work and, at special occasions, caters to the inflatable Flower.

Water Line

Water is an element used throughout the work. The water line charges the steam generator, cools the laser, provides water to form ice on the brine line and supplies the water prism. It also produces water events along the water pipe in the form of fans of mist emitting from high-pressure nozzles.

Sound/Communications Line

Recorded instrumental, vocal and electronic music which has been subjected to multiple time-displacement processing is played back at irregular times through a series of loudspeakers placed along "Centerbeam". The system consists of an 8-track audiocartridge tape deck supplying a high-quality quadraphonic signal to standard music-quality amplifiers. The system also draws upon short- and long-wave radio transmissions, public and private, and therefore requires antennae and receivers to be built into "Centerbeam", in addition to the multiplexing electronics specifically assembled for these radio signals. Two-second samples of each radio signal are sequenced so that new composite language emerges. The system changes periodically and can be varied by the spectator.

Video Reflection

Live television images of the participant/viewers of "Centerbeam" are mixed with pre-arranged, programmed images originating from American standard ¾-inch video cassette machines to appear, via coaxial cable, on television monitors dug into the ground near "Centerbeam". A variable controlled-interval timer records and recalls pictures of "Centerbeam" and people around it.

By using a cassette editor/player as a memory device, alternate-play commands and insert-edit commands are issued to the continuously recycling machine controlled by coincident—multivibrator oscillations. The result is a collage of time-shifted images ranging from the shortest delay, equal to one programmed tape cycle, to delays of varying lengths. Older images are replaced with more recent images in a pseudo-random checkerboard array.

"Centerbeam"
documenta 6
poetry (Mark Mendel)
photograph:
Dietmar Loehrl

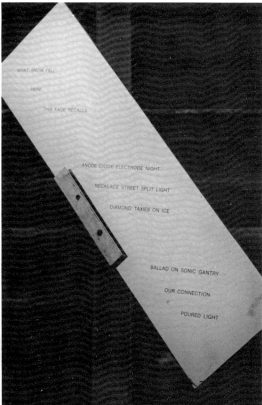

"Centerbeam"
documenta 6
poetry on mirror
(Mark Mendel)
photograph:
Dietmar Loehrl

Poetry Line

The poetry line consists of the 102-line *Poem On,*[4] silhouette-screened with mirroring silver onto eight glass rectangles, each 28" x 8". 180° swivel mounts allow viewers to manipulate the mirrors which also reflect the surroundings and the readers' faces. Poem mounts are located on the stanchions above the water prism so that when the angle of sunlight is perpendicular to the mirror face, the glass acts as a stencil, "writing" or "casting" the poem on the water surface.

Grow Line

The grow line features fast-growing seasonal vegetation. It provides counterpoint to the technology of other lines. Vegetation grows out of open ceramic troughs.

"Centerbeam", D.C.
detail of water prism and
kalliroscopic "White River"
(Paul Matisse)
photograph:
Calvin Campbell/M.I.T.

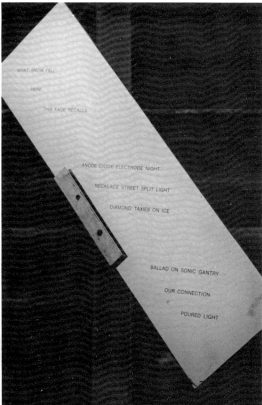

"Centerbeam", D.C.
detail of "Drawing With
Your Eyes" device
(Derith Glover)
photograph: Jeanne Coffin

Drawing with Your Eyes

The Drawing with Your Eyes machine, designed as a therapeutic as well as artistic tool, is one of the participatory stations along "Centerbeam". The apparatus uses the moving pupil to reflect a pencil beam as a "drawing light". The reflected beam is picked up by a video camera and transmitted to a delay-burn video screen and thus displays a "continuous" drawing which remains on the screen for several seconds and can be photographed.

Kalliroscopic "White River"

A "white river" of enveloped kalliroscopic fluid runs underneath the water prism reflecting sunlight and the sun spectra emanating from the water prism. It is a current of gentle turbulences, evanescent yet part of a continuum. As visitors touch the "white river" surface they modify the patterns of its flow.

60

"Centerbeam", D.C.
detail of steam
(Joan Brigham)
photograph:
Calvin Campbell/M.I.T.

"Centerbeam", D.C.
detail of "Sound Shuffle"/
"Light Walk"
(Chris Janney)
photograph:
Calvin Campbell/M.I.T.

Events and Performances

"Centerbeam" is a performing sculpture as well as stage and stage set with machinery for events and performances. Certain performances are scheduled on a regular daily or nightly basis; others are single performances.

Planned spectacles include elemental events combining ice, steam, water-spray and compressed air; the appearance of big, floating inflatables such as a black rose. Regularly scheduled performances feature laser and film projections on steam clouds and flying sculptures ("sky flowers"). Theatric productions include the sky opera "Icarus" and the fairy-tale opera "Bremen Town Musicians", using large, floating, inflatable costumes, laser imagery, live singers and musicians, and amplifying sound and light media.[5]

[1] 19 stanchions support the entire "Centerbeam", i.e., the water prism and all the pipe lines stacked diagonally above it.
[2] "White" is used in quotation marks because all individual colors are present in this white laser in unequal intensities. The dominant line is one of several wave-lengths of green light, and it "colors" the white.
[3] Brine is a close-to-saturated salt/water solution.
[4] By C.A.V.S. Fellow Mark Mendel.
[5] "Icarus"—not "Bremen Town Musicians"—was produced in D.C.

"Centerbeam", D.C.
laser projections (Paul Earls)
on steam (Joan Brigham)
photograph: K.M. Kiely

"Centerbeam", D.C.
with "Brussels Flower" sky
event (Otto Piene)
photograph:
Elizabeth Goldring

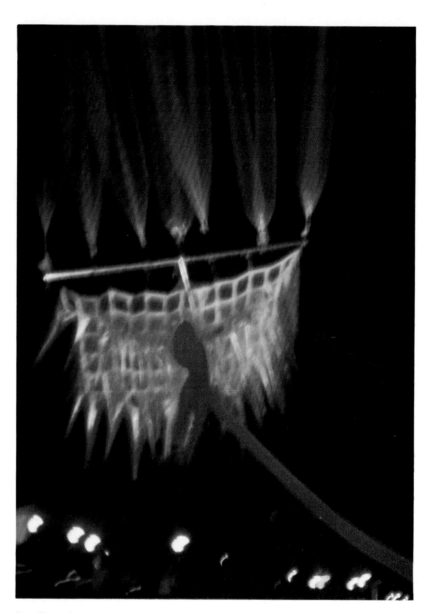

Otto Piene, Icarus
for sky opera, "Icarus"
(Earls, Piene)
"Centerbeam", D.C.
September, 1978
photograph:
Elizabeth Goldring

"Centerbeam", D.C.
detail of steam
(Joan Brigham)
photograph:
Calvin Campbell/M.I.T.

Joan Brigham

Steam

"Just as water, gas and electricity are brought into our houses from far off to satisfy our needs in response to minimal efforts, so we shall be supplied with visual and auditory images which will appear and disappear at a simple movement of the hand, hardly more than a sign."

(Paul Valéry, *Aesthetics: The Conquest of Ubiquity,* translated by Ralph Manheim, Pantheon Books, Bollingen Series, New York, 1964, p. 225)

Steam suggests various analogies. Like other energy systems, it has no fixed form. Hovering between visibility and invisibility, it exhorts a relativist view of reality. Interacting by transparent expansion in the surrounding environment, it transmutes appearance to apparition; presence to absence.

It makes visible temperature, wind velocity and directions, humidity, and light. Like other forms of air art, it fulfills a directive by Merleau-Ponty: "No more is it a question of speaking of space and light; the question is to make the space and light which is there, speak to us."

Surfaces, distances, planes, textures, scale—the factors by which we orient ourselves in space—hover like ghosts in mid-air. Steam enters the space like a dancer onstage, and energizes that space through continuous movement. When the movement ceases, a void appears. I conceive of steam work, like the dance, as an event of specific duration and am in agreement with Willoughby Sharp: "Reality is energy, not things. Reality is events, not objects."

Prior to my arrival at the *documenta* site, I had conducted a series of experiments with steam systems for the determined 144-foot length of "Centerbeam". These were executed with both electric and gas-fired generators in order to establish exact specifications for the type of steam generator to be used in Kassel.

When the conceptual phases of "Centerbeam" were concluded, it was my sense that the steam line needed to perform two different functions: 1) to bathe the work in a wide horizontal plane of steam spiraling most of its length; 2) to provide a dense cloud of steam extending at least 30 feet above the pipeline, to receive the laser beam and laser-projected images.

In the first instance, a steam pressure of 20 psi would suffice; in the latter, a pressure of 60-80 psi was needed. Although both pressures could be supplied by a single generator, two independent but parallel piping and valving systems were

69

needed. Thus, the specification was for a generator with a wide range of pressures, capable of maintaining constant pressure for several hours a day. Moreover, the length of the steam line, 20 meters (8 sections) required that a minimum of 2" pipe be used, since smaller pipe would increase pressure drop because of increased friction on the inside pipe walls. An ordinary pressure drop in a 2" pipe line is 1 lb. per 100 linear feet, but because the spiral configuration required small holes drilled along its entire length, the pressure drop would increase relative to a summation of the orifice equation. The size of the holes, 2 mm., causes the hole to act as a tube, reducing the interior steam pressure so it emerges at atmospheric pressure and condenses instantly. This eliminates the danger of superheated, invisible steam.

The second system was designed to provide 4 vertical jets of steam. Each opening was tapped by a reducing valve, 2" x ¾" at 4 points equidistant along the 20 meter length. The height of each plume could then be adjusted to the laser beam aimed along the length of the work, 8-10' above it and at a slight incline.

The location of the feed line from the generator at the 13th stanchion was important in order to create even distribution of the steam from that point towards either end. With this entry point, the vertical plumes of the spiral occurred at an area far enough in front of the last stanchion so that the curve could be clearly distinguished as rising and falling the full 20 meters of the line.

I was fortunate to acquire a generator in Kassel of 2000 kg per hour, which could be adjusted within a range of 16-25 atmospheres. This enabled both systems to be sensitively responsive to hourly changes of atmospheric conditions and artistic whim.

The steam lines for "Centerbeam" D.C. were arranged in a somewhat different configuration: the spiral line of steam was positioned at the apex of the water prism in order to more completely "float" the work. The individual jets were replaced by 12 solenoid valves located on the topmost section of the structure in order for the steam to intercept the laser images along its entire length. These valves were wired to a key-board so that members of the audience could "play" the solenoids. The change from ordinary valves to solenoids proved more satisfactory for two reasons: the jets of steam were emitted in a more unpredictable and spontaneous way and, second, the keyboard encouraged further audience participation during performances.

Kassel was an appropriate location for the first large-scale use of steam in environmental art. It was here that Denis Papin, encouraged by the success of his "Digester"—the first steam cooker, constructed a steam generator capable of propelling boat oars. Papin and his family along with Baron von Hesse navigated the Fulda River adjacent to the Baron's property, and, to Papin's delight, the boat travelled as competently upstream as downstream.

Because of the unstable political climate at Kassel, Papin was obliged to leave. Unable to obtain permission to navigate his boat, even through Leibnitz's efforts, Papin departed aboard his steamship. It ran aground, and while he was repairing it, the boat was seized by the local authorities, partially destroyed, and the parts sold at public auction. Papin did arrive at his destination— England—the following year and presented evidence of his steamboat to the Royal Academy of London, of which Sir Isaac Newton was then president. An inscription on the Ottoneum in Kassel reads:

"Denis Papin, der Erfinder der Dampfmaschine, hat auf diesem Platze in Gegenwart des Landgrafen Karl von Hessen im Juni 1706 die ersten grösseren Versuche mit Anwendung der Dampfkraft erfolgreich ausgeführt."

(Trans.: Denis Papin, the inventor of the steam engine, conducted the first major tests here for the successful use of steampower. This took place in June, 1706 in the presence of Baron Karl von Hesse.)

Otto Piene
"Neon Rainbow"
with Alejandro Sina
Briggs Field, M.I.T.
Cambridge, Massachusetts
1975
photograph:
Calvin Campbell/M.I.T.

Alejandro Sina

Neon-Argon Line

A sculptural light component of "Centerbeam", the neon-argon line points towards dreams of large-scale kinetic works using electrical gas discharge phenomena. Single induction electrodes, a high-frequency power supply, and parallel, single-line wiring are improvements over the series and double-conductor wiring of traditional neon sign technology. These techniques permit lightweight, nearly invisible wiring and rigging, making more feasible the use of helium gas balloons as carriers for night sky events and large-scale sculptures.

My work for "Centerbeam" should be considered in the context of two recent projects. The first was the "Neon Rainbow", technically described as a 300-foot-long helium balloon carrying seventy units, each two feet in length. This event had both day and night aspects. I developed it together with Otto Piene who had previously realized his helium balloon, incandescent light rainbows. The second project was my permanent installation in a public, indoor space of a large, kinetic sculpture.[1] This argon "needle cluster" consists of 108 feet of glass tubes filled with argon gas, positioned along three suspended 90-foot lines.

The "Neon Rainbow" showed that neon glass tubes would operate beautifully along linear runs of at least 140 feet. The complete electrical rigging weighed less than 10 pounds and power consumption was below 50 watts. The "Neon Rainbow" proved the large-scale feasibility of these techniques.

The "needle cluster" has been glowing without interruption for many months. It has confirmed the electrical/mechanical reliability of the system as a whole. This system with its lightweight rigging and ultra-low power consumption has advanced traditional neon technology.

The neon-argon line for "Centerbeam" consists of two 144-foot long parallel lines inside a glass tube four inches in diameter. The 300 linear feet of blue and red light is almost twice the footage of the "Neon Rainbow". I am experimenting with a modified wiring/electrical design which makes the lines glow red and blue in controlled patterns. Their mingling with the lights and water prism reflections increases their illusive magic. Wind generates the power for the neon-argon line.

I hope that the "Centerbeam" experience will spur realization of other artists' dreams which use electricity and technology in an expressly kinetic and visual manner.

[1] In the Hyatt Regency Hotel in Cambridge, Massachusetts.

71

Paul Earls
laser projected image
"Bird" (Otto Piene)
photograph:
Mennerich/McCann

Paul Earls

Laser and Music/Sound Lines

My contributions to "Centerbeam"—the laser lines and music/sound lines—are an outgrowth of my association with stage-directed media events using both idioms. For me "Centerbeam" is a public "grand opera". It is designed to communicate with its audience in simultaneous modes and with many voices. Fantastic and real are juxtaposed. Backstage is onstage. Its specific idiom is American, ranging from the shy and ethereal to the boisterous and aggressive and from the equivocal to the solidly tangible. The various media and dimensions of sensibility are finally inseparable, yet individually appreciable.

The laser systems alternate between the simple prismatic spreading of a multi-colored beam and computer-generated images projected on steam, trees, and buildings. The scale of projected images is infinitely variable.

Laser projections have been used by artists and composers for over a decade. The technique is simple: the thin laser beam, seen as a dot when it is projected onto a surface, is successively directed to two moving mirrors, one for the horizontal and one for the vertical plane. Patterns of light are produced because the dot moves rapidly enough for the eye to see continuous lines, just as rapid clicks are heard by the ear as a continuous tone.

When the mirrors are glued to loudspeakers (or otherwise vibrated by music) music automatically produces a visual mathematical analogue of itself.

Precise mathematical relationships between the rate of movement of the two mirrors result in simple geometrical shapes (Lissajous figures) such as the circle (1:1—a musical unison) and the figure-eight (2:1—a musical octave). More complex relationships produce correspondingly intricate patterns. If these relationships are not exact (i.e., slightly out of tune), the pattern will slowly rotate at the beat frequency (the difference rate between perfect tuning and actuality). This event creates a compelling visual illusion: a floating, rotating "media sculpture".

I first used computers with lasers in the spring of 1974, with Stan Knutson, an M.I.T. undergraduate and systems programmer for the Joint Computer Facility. We replaced loudspeakers with galvanometers, sensitive and accurate enough to receive and reproduce precise, minute, varying voltages supplied by the computer. Images were created by drawing with a light-pen (a clumsy technique for visual artists) or by feeding in x-y coordinants on punched cards or paper tape. Once created and edited for the galvanometer-controlled scanners, these images use existing or new software within the computer for image variations such as re-scaling, dimensional rotation, etc.

72

Paul Earls
laser projected image
"Snow Goose" (Otto Piene)
photograph:
Mennerich/McCann

That early work was supported by a grant from the National Endowment for the Arts. It required a medium-size computer and its peripherals: about $90,000 of equipment.

Our demands for complex imagery quickly exceeded the capability of reasonably priced encoding techniques for display away from the computer so we replaced encoded audio tape with a small, portable, on-line computer. In the spring of 1977, Michael Burns, an M.I.T. graduate student in spectroscopy, developed our first programs for an 8080 microprocessor with eight kilobytes of memory. This system went with "Centerbeam" to Kassel, with a back-up library of FM encoded tapes. On-line animation is a feature of this system. Each point of the images has to be continuously fed to the scanners, and thus, each or all points can be altered as the program runs. For example, the opening and closing of Gyorgy Kepes' envelope image require that the points defining the peaks of the envelope's flap "move" on successive displays of the image. The speed and amount of that change are selected by the operator. The Kassel "Centerbeam" images were drawn on graph paper, crucial points determined, calculated, and typed into the computer in hexadecimal machine code. Movement was entered in the same manner, and a simple animation system (MOVE, in assembly language) was created. It was accurate and dependable, but difficult to use.

Alva Couch, an undergraduate M.I.T. composer with extensive computer experience, created a new multi-environmental editing language, MORPHASE, in time for "Centerbeam" D.C. This system has the ability to draw and edit imagery on-line with the laser. It is a powerful and flexible system. Some versions have letters of the alphabet on file so that messages can be typed directly onto the laser display via the computer keyboard.

Early lasers were relatively weak, expensive, and limited in color. The "Centerbeam" laser, a 4-watt mixed gas (argon and krypton) laser contains twelve different colors within its beam. The unseparated beam is greenish-white, and is used for animated imagery projections on steam screens, trees or buildings. When directed through a prism, all of the colors fan out, spreading over nine feet at the end of "Centerbeam". The steam passes in and out of this stationary spectral fan like a visual Morse Code—the light becomes substantial, material and active. Imagery projected into steam is unexpectedly transformed. In addition to the envelope we used geometrical and celestial patterns as well as human hand-sketched forms (eyes, mouth, hand) and words.

The interaction of music, laser and other spectacles was a nightly feature of the "Centerbeam"

D.C. performances which culminated in two
presentations of *Icarus,* the sky opera Otto Piene
and I created. In *Icarus,* "Centerbeam" itself was
a character (the Minotaur) composed of steam,
hand-drawn laser projections representing an eye,
mouth, bull's head, birds. There was taped and
live music along with an inflatable flying sculpture,
Icarus, and a performer in the sky (Daedalus). In
this context the laser became integrated with other
media and performers in an environmental drama.

What will happen next now that high-power multi-
color lasers, of search-light brilliance, are available?
Laser projections will undoubtedly become
wedded to holography, creating new theater
spaces and large-scale public communication and
entertainment possibilities. Perhaps there will be
some truly interesting sound-light work by composers and visual artists who perceive laser work
as an expanded musical gesture. Opera has tradi-
tionally embodied the dramatic marriage of
content, media and music. Perhaps opera and
other staged media may once again evolve into a
new, highly dynamic environmental theatrical
medium of 20th-century expression, utilizing new
instruments of current technology, such as film,
video, electronic music, computers—and laser.

Harriet Casdin-Silver
hologram, "Equivocal Forks"
for "Centerbeam"
documenta 6
photograph: Dietmar Loehrl

Harriet Casdin-Silver

"Centerbeam" *documenta 6* —
"Centerbeam" Washington, D.C.

I will try to share some of my experiences as holographic artist for both events. The first section contains excerpts from notations made throughout the process of creating the holography line and its solar tracking components for "Centerbeam", *documenta 6.*

The Beginning — January 1977

Holograms — solar-tracked — the sun will be the light source — a series of 12½" x 16½" plates — imagery about 3' (one meter) projected frontally — scale bigger, brighter for outside — plates must be sealed, to protect the emulsion from the elements. Holograms have never been exhibited outside, nor have they been illuminated by sun-tracking devices.

The imagery must integrate with the overall "Centerbeam" concept, but also act as a dichotomy. Holograms will be extensions/arms of the stanchions, reaching out, beckoning, enticing the spectator/participant. The transmission[1] "forks" I am working on in my laboratory[2] ("real" image; pseudoscopic[3]) will generate white-light transmission holograms[4] — still pseudoscopic, recognizable but holographic, containing extensive visual variation with the movement of the spectator. Positive and negative space will fuse and separate, causing kinetic equivocal interplay. Colors will also change; with either the sun or electric light as the reconstructing source, the spectral coloration is inherent in the system. Each hologram will be seen in one color at a time, each color dependent on the spectator's viewing angle and angle of the sun or light source. Dichotomy will exist in the holograms themselves as well as in their relation to our total structure. Under particular lighting circumstances, phallic prongs thrusting at the viewer project hostility. As pseudoscopic equivocal forks, however, they turn themselves around, prongs away from the viewer.

Mid-Way — March 1977

I remind myself that we at the Center for Advanced Visual Studies attempt feats that neither scientists nor engineers would consider undertaking with such minimal funding — and we produce.

The imagery is working well, but there are unresolved complexities of presentation — for example, the sun will cause blurring of image if image is not close to the plate; the sun will not always be a viable light source, I must use a light for cloudy days and at night. (One day we will store solar energy in a capsule to "turn on" when the sun goes down.) Can we really protect the holographic emulsion from the elements? The visual definition

of the forks is hurt by the sun and by the most intense lamps — the more intensity, the less definition — the more definition, the less intensity. If the image is not bright and crisp, it simply does not "hang out" there in space. But we are still mid-way. We shall solve these problems. Our M.I.T. physicist-astronomer[5] is developing an apparently "elegant" system which can be used anywhere in the world.

Opening — June 24, 1977

We are opening up environmental holographic possibilities formerly unattainable. Scale and color are limitations still to be overcome. We must beware of the "beer bottle in the sky" mentality — the risk exists.

"Centerbeam II" — Washington, D.C.

The Washington, D.C. "Centerbeam" gave me an opportunity to refine and perfect the system. The solar-tracking electronics were adjusted[6] to afford sun-illumination of the holograms for longer periods of the day. They were less affected by clouds blocking the sun. For sunless days and night reconstruction, more intense lamp-illumination was devised.[7]

The "Equivocal Forks" were reconstructed by the solar trackers at the angle for which they were designed, and again by the sun's beams directly, without the intervention of the trackers. Thereby an ever-changing multitude of forks appeared. The brightness of the holograms was such that the forks floated out to either side of the plates.

To be fully experienced, the holograms, like the rest of "Centerbeam", had to be seen at different times from many vantage points — in the sunlight, at night, at close range, from a distance; through trees, people, energy lines and pipes of "Centerbeam". The forks emerged through the steam, tentatively, one at a time, until the steam disappeared and they were all visible in concert — "Gabeln!"; "Wo sind sie?"; "Forks! Where are they?"

[1] Holography is a method of producing an accurate three-dimensional image via the coherent light of the laser. For me, as an artist, it is sculpture of light, floating in space. The information recorded in the holographic emulsion is reconstructed with the appropriate spatial relationships possessed by any three-dimensional object or light formation.

Transmission holography is the basic holographic system: the laser beam is split; one or more beams light the object; another, called the reference beam, is directed toward the holographic plate or film. The reference beam, spread or diverged by a lens to cover the plate, and the light waves from the object reach the plate at the same time. This causes an interference pattern which results in the recording of the light from the object in the holographic emulsion. After exposure, the plate is developed in the "darkroom" — a process similar to photography.

To form the image in space, a "reconstructing reference" beam must be directed toward the plate at the same angle as the "reference" in exposure, meeting again the information now stored in the emulsion.

Transmission holograms are produced and reconstructed by laser light. A mercury arc lamp may be used for reconstruction, but the laser affords more defined imagery.

[2] In 1976-77 I was functioning at both M.I.T. and Brown University; I created the transmission holograms at my Brown University laboratory, Providence, Rhode Island. Lab assistants: Donald Thornton and Gordon Cates.

[3] The term "real" image generally refers to the image projected in front of the holographic plate or film; "pseudoscopic" image refers to the image perceptively "turned inside out" (for example, the fork prongs as they were constructed on the holographic table and as "virtual" image face the spectator and are seen behind the plate; the "real", pseudoscopic forks reconstruct themselves in front of the plate, prongs traveling away from the spectator).

[4] At the time of this writing, white-light transmission holograms are second generation holograms made by lasers but reconstructed by white light — the sun in our case — rather than laser light. In the holographic system, a "slit" of light on the master transmission plate, containing all the image-information, is exposed to a second plate which will be the white-light transmission hologram.

[5] Dr. Walter Lewin, assisted by Michael Naimark, Brian Raila and Kenneth Kantor.

[6] By Kenneth Kantor.

[7] By Donald Thornton.

Holography Line: Special Technical Requirements for "Centerbeam"

8 hologram plates, 12½"x16½", project imagery frontally toward the viewer. They are white light transmission holograms which use the sun or, when necessary, an illuminator as their light source. Illumination is from a white light point source (3000° K) behind and above each hologram at a distance of two meters at a 45° angle. The point of light should have an angular distance of no greater than 1/6° horizontally and 2° vertically. Each holographic image appears in one color at a time, depending on the viewer's angle and the angle of the light source. The holograms are laminated to protective glass, placed level with the top edges of the water prism and spaced to agree with other "Centerbeam" activities. The holograms contain imagery that is perceived realistically, but projected frontally in space about 3 feet. Extensive visual variation occurs with movement both of the spectator and of the sun. Positive and negative space interact, fuse, and separate, causing kinetic equivocal interplay between the spectator and the images.

Certain holograms are solar-tracked using a servo controlled solar-tracking system. A 60° arc of a 40 cm cylindrical mirror is mounted on a vertical axis at the required distance and angle from each hologram. Although such mirrors weaken the reflected sunlight cylindrical mirrors have two important advantages: 1) the curvature of the cylinder eliminates the need to track in the horizontal dimension; and 2) the horizontal

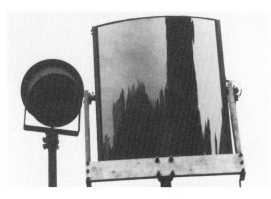

solar mirror
for "Centerbeam"
documenta 6
photograph: Dietmar Loehrl

angular distance of the sun is required from 1/2° to less than 1/6°.

Solar tracking is required only in the vertical dimension. The cylindrical mirrors must rock back and forth in their axis. The rocking motion is achieved by a two-directional motor, controlled by a pan of photocells mounted near the bottom edge of each hologram. A logic circuit directs the motor until the photocells sense light and the hologram is illuminated. When there is not sufficient sunlight, power is transferred from the servo system to a halogen cycle quartz spotlamp.

Comment on Solar Tracking

My concept for solar illumination of the holograms on "Centerbeam" was stimulated by the following factors. 1) "Centerbeam," for me, is essentially an energy beam. 2) If the holograms are specifically designed to use the sun, the sun can be a brilliant light source. Sun energy to light outdoor holograms is a plausible and exciting treatment for this special situation. 3) I hope eventually to store the sun. The holograms then could be illuminated by sunlight at night.

While the solar-tracking system was being designed for the holograms, aesthetic considerations remained of primary importance. The design, materials and installation of the cylindrical mirrors had to integrate with "Centerbeam" itself as well as with the holograms. The mirrors and other devices could not be allowed to detract from the holographic imagery.

Walter H. G. Lewin
Stephen Benton
Jim Ballintine
Patricia Downey
Kenneth Kantor
Michael Naimark
Brian Raila

Solar Tracking of Holograms for "Centerbeam"

Our objectives were to design and build a system that would allow solar illumination (using mirrors) of Harriet Casdin-Silver's holograms for "Centerbeam" in Kassel, Germany. The "solar tracking" had to be automatic and it had to provide enough light for the holograms between June and October, 1977.

In this paper we describe how our ideas evolved and how we arrived at a simple design for the solar trackers.

In what follows, whenever we use the word 'image' we mean the image of the sun formed by a mirror. Whenever we talk about the image formed by the hologram, which is the final product (Harriet's creation) that the bystanders see, we will say 'holographic-image'.

A sketch of a hologram, the light incident to it and the location of the holographic-image is shown in figure 1. Seven such systems were present in Kassel. The holograms were specially designed to produce the holographic-image of the forks if a white light source illuminated the holograms at a 45° angle from the vertical. Our task was to design and construct a mirror system that would reflect a beam of light from the sun onto the holograms so that the above condition would be met independently of the position of the sun in the sky. We examined the possibility of using flat mirrors, convex mirrors and cylindrical mirrors.

Flat Mirrors

Flat mirrors have the advantage that when a beam of light reflects, there are almost no losses in light intensity. When you look at the sun in a flat mirror you see almost the same amount of reflected sunlight as when you look straight at the sun.

Astronomers have tracked the sun for decades in solar observatories using two flat mirrors, one stationary and one rotating about a polar axis. This 'classic' double mirror system causes the reflected sunlight to enter the observatory in the same direction. Thus, we could have used this 'classic' scheme for our purpose. However, if we had done so, just as in solar observatories, the stationary mirror would have had to be moved to a different location about twice a week. In the case of the "Centerbeam" holograms, in a period of 3 months this mirror would have had to be moved by several meters! In addition, one of the two mirrors would have had to be mounted a few meters away from "Centerbeam" either up in the air (clumsy-looking mounting support) or on the ground (interfering with people). Therefore, this scheme was rejected as highly impractical and very

expensive, and we looked into the possibility of using only *one* flat mirror.

In principle, for a given position of the sun, one flat mirror can always be oriented to reflect the light rays onto the hologram at the desired angle (45° from the vertical). Imagine that the mirror is mounted at a fixed position somewhere along the line HM (figure 1), and let the sun be at position S somewhere in the sky. When the line perpendicular to the mirror is the bisector of the angle SMH, we satisfy the required condition (light rays from the sun will reflect off the mirror in the direction of the hologram). With the sun moving in the sky, obviously the mirror's orientation (not its location) has to be changed; this is where the "tracking" part comes in.

In order for the mirror to find its own proper orientation automatically it could perform a raster scan. When the light rays from the sun (reflected off the mirror) strike the hologram the reflected beam could automatically "lock" onto the hologram (photo diodes mounted on the hologram would sense the beam and command the raster scan to stop). In this scheme a mirror motion about 2 axes is required (i.e., a rotation of the mirror about a vertical and a horizontal axis). Every time clouds passed over the sun, however, it could take up to 30 minutes for the beam to engage again. Thus, on a day with scattered clouds, the tracking system would be searching for the proper orientation of the mirror most of the time. We therefore rejected this scheme and in order to simplify the tracking, we decided to look into the possibility of using convex mirrors.

Convex Mirrors

If you place a crystal ball (used by fortune tellers) outside, you can see almost everything around you and above you, reflected in the sphere. (In Europe people used to put such crystal balls in their gardens.) Looking into the ball, one can see the sun for most of the day. Therefore, if a convex mirror which is a portion of our crystal ball (used on motorcycles to see what is behind the rider) is placed somewhere along the line HM (figure 1), sunlight would be reflected onto the hologram most of the day without moving the mirror, and thus no tracking device would be needed! This, of course, is a very appealing approach. However, it is easy to see that a convex mirror which reflects the light in all directions, does not provide as strong a light beam for the holograms as flat mirrors which reflect the sunlight in one direction only. To further pursue the possibility of using a convex mirror, it was essential for us to know how weak the reflected light beam could be in order to get a good quality holographic-image. We performed a simple experiment using direct sunlight

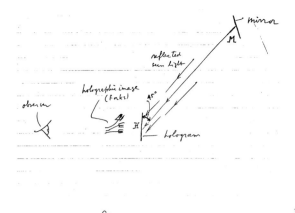

Figure 1

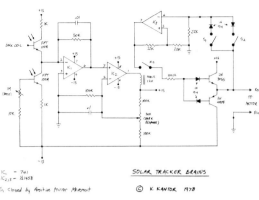

IC₁ – 741
IC₂,₃ – ½ 1453

S₁ Closed by Positive Mirror Movement

SOLAR TRACKER BRAINS

© K. KANTOR 1978

Walter Lewin
figure 1

Kenneth Kantor
figure 2

and filters. A light beam approximately twenty times fainter than we receive directly from the sun would still be adequate but one about 40 times fainter would not work. In using convex mirrors, it can be shown that the light in comparison with a flat mirror is reduced by a factor $\sim \frac{4L^2}{R^2}$ (for R<L). Here L is the distance from the hologram to the mirror (HM in figure 1) and R is the radius of curvature of the convex mirror. Thus, a necessary condition is: $\frac{4L^2}{R^2} < 20$ from which it follows that R> 0.4L. If L is about 2 meters, the radius of the mirror R would have to be at least about 1 meter. This might not be a problem by itself; however, it can be shown independently that the size (diameter) of a convex mirror has to be equal to the radius of curvature of the mirror if one wants to avoid the complication of mirror motion (tracking). We realized that the purchase of convex mirrors of this size (one meter across) would exceed our budget limitations. We therefore abandoned the idea of using convex mirrors and we explored the possibility of using a cylindrical mirror instead.

Cylindrical Mirrors

It can easily be shown that solar tracking with one cylindrical mirror requires rotation of the mirror about one axis only (as opposed to two axes for a flat mirror and zero axes for a convex mirror). A one-axis tracking system using photo diodes as described above could be quite simple. If rotation about only one axis is required, the search for the light beam to lock onto the hologram would take no more than one minute, which is acceptable even if scattered clouds frequently interrupt the solar rays.

The reduction of light from a cylindrical mirror in comparison with a flat mirror is of order $\frac{L}{R}$ (here, R is the radius of curvature of the cylinder). Thus with $\frac{L}{R} < 20 \rightarrow R > \frac{L}{20}$ with L=2 meter, R >0.1 m (= 10cm).

This is considerably smaller and therefore more practical than the 1 meter that we found earlier for the convex mirror.

There is a fundamental difference between the solar image formed by a flat mirror or a convex mirror and that of a cylindrical mirror. If you look at the image of the sun in either a flat or a convex mirror and move your head around, the solar image will *not* move. However, if you look at the sun in a cylindrical mirror, while moving your head around, the image *will* move along a line parallel to the center line (axis) of the cylinder; the solar images lie on a straight line.

Fortunately with the proper orientation of the holograms, the holographic-image (forks) can be seen with a narrow line-shaped source of light such as is produced by a cylindrical mirror.

A cylindrical mirror has two additional advantages over flat mirrors. The line image of the sun formed by a cylindrical mirror is substantially narrower than the 0.5° size of the sun which would

Table 1: Some Details of Tracking System

overall dimensions of mirror mount	21.5" high, 19" wide, 4" deep
weight	~ 15 lbs
frame material	aluminum
size holograms	12.5" high, 16.5" wide
distance hologram to mirror	~ 200 cm
mirror dimensions	18" high, ~ 16" across
mirror radius	40 cm (L/R = 5)
mirror material	aluminized plexiglass (~ 90% reflectivity)
motor	Globe, 12V DC, ~ 200 mA, ~ 1 rpm

figure 3
Cylindrical mirror
with back up illuminator
photograph:
Dietmar Loehrl

figure 4
Solar tracking mirror
photograph:
Dietmar Loehrl

be the width of the solar image had flat mirrors been used. (The narrower the light source, the higher the quality of the holographic image.) The second advantage of the cylindrical mirror is the fact that the virtual solar image formed is located slightly behind the surface of the mirror. In other words, the solar image is located only a little over 2 meters from the hologram. If a flat mirror had been used, the image would have been at 'infinity' (as the sun itself). Harriet Casdin-Silver also wanted artificial lights to show the holograms at night. The distance between the artificial lights and the holograms would be 2 meters. A hologram designed to be illuminated by a light source at a 2-meter distance will not work well holographically if the light source is moved substantially further away. Therefore, had flat mirrors been used during the day, the same holograms could not have been used both night and day; however, with cylindrical mirrors the same holograms can be used.

Once we realized that with a cylindrical mirror everything seemed to 'click', we zeroed in on our final design very quickly.

Final Design

Figure 3 shows a picture (taken at Kassel) of a cylindrical mirror with a back-up illuminator. A close-up picture of a mirror and its frame containing the motor is shown in figure 4. Table 1 gives some technical details on the tracking system. A simple servo feed-back system controls the mirror motion (see figure 2). Two photo diodes are mounted on the hologram, one on top and one at the bottom.

The circuit has two states: (i) if both photocells are properly illuminated, the mirror is held stationary; (ii) otherwise, the mirror scans back and forth until both cells are correctly illuminated. A simple memory system eliminates the need to perform a full search every time the sun moves out of the field of one of the cells.

The tracking systems were designed so that they will work not only in Kassel, Germany, but anywhere on Earth. Four systems were installed in Kassel, by mid-June, 1977; three additional mirrors could be aimed manually by the spectator/participants.

81

Elizabeth Goldring

The Sky Events — Piene's Flying Sculptures

Vital to the cumulative success of our "Center-beam" presentation on the National Mall were Otto Piene's 23 sky events and the launching of his red Icarus, and manned helium sculpture, Daedalus, prepared for the sky odyssey-opera, *Icarus* (Paul Earls and Otto Piene). His flying black roses, red anemones and star flowers appeared periodically at the "Centerbeam" site in dialogue with laser projections, steam and elec-tronic music. The flying sculptures festooned "the beast" and fastened "Centerbeam" to its very location — making the work tangibly site-specific in many ways. The vertical thrust expanded the scale of "Centerbeam", at the same time punctu-ating the widely horizontal axis of the Mall. The soft fabrics and "natural" forms provided contrast to the hardware of "Centerbeam" and the hard edge treatment of Mall buildings and boulevards. The softly responsive gestures of Piene's sky flowers complemented the computer-programmed anima-tion of laser-drawn images, and anticipated and recorded the movement of light breezes circulating about the space. The brightly lighted, intensely colored sculptures lent surrealist drama and beauty to the stark magnificence of this generous and important stage set. The highly visible, readable images became immediately accessible parts of "Centerbeam" — public art as commonly experi-ential as kite flying, as exhilarating as ascending balloons, as "real" as any art but constantly moving and changing, enticing people to see, stay and play along.

The sky events generated participating enthusi-asms of the sort that museum educators have been trying to achieve in recent "participative" exhibits. Participants included fellow artists, public and museum officials, passers-by and "repeats".

The sky events occurred frequently because of Piene's personal commitment. (He directed each event and supervised the maintenance of his existing sculptures and the fabrication of new sculptures in our navyyard workshop.)

The recurring sky events were also made possible by a generous helium donation from the Gardner Cryogenics Division of Phillips Petroleum Company, an abundance of good weather and the continuing cooperation of air traffic authorities.

Flying art precedents on the Mall are rare. They include Piene's Washington Sky Ballet executed on May 16, 1970, and the ascension of an occa-sional balloon. Piene had hoped to fly his "Milwaukee Anemone" from the roof of the National Air and Space Museum for additional sculptural/architectural comment on this location.

82

The plan was thwarted not by air traffic laws but by building safety codes. His subsequent "safe operations" and successes with flying sculptures from buildings—the Secession in Vienna, Austria; the County Building on Calder Plaza in Grand Rapids, Michigan; and the twelve story library at the University of Guadalajara, Mexico—may encourage Smithsonian officials to reconsider. The Smithsonian museums and the Mall itself would be one excellent location for the forthcoming sky art conference — a C.A.V.S./M.I.T. enterprise under Piene's direction.

The sky art conference will happen at many locations in the U.S. and abroad, offering a confluence of events, performances, lectures, symposia, and publications—by artists, public officials, sky sports enthusiasts, scientists, writers, corporations, and "all others" active in the sky.

A brief comment by Piene on sky art follows:

"My first sky events were modest and only conceptually 'mine'. They were part of the Group Zero 'demonstrations' in Europe in 1961/62. They inspired further use of air techniques and increasing scale. The growing size made them more public, and the growing public demand made them bigger — leading to such pieces as the 1,600-foot "Olympic Rainbow" in Munich, 1972. Out

of indoor pieces ("Red Rapid Growth" in Pittsburgh, 1970) came the 'flying flowers' ("Milwaukee Anemone", "Brussels Flower", "Black Rose", "Icarus"), and "Carousel" is a combination of Icarus and Anemone. Although the sky sculptures are soft and 'organic' the underlying formal principle is 'constructivist', geometric, 'geodesic' ("Iowa Star"). The dimensions (ca. 250 feet of height when fully inflated and flying) suggest public, participatory affairs to be occasions and festive spirit to generate the energies necessary for a day-and-night sky event. More than any indoor art, sky events promote interplay between people, objets d'art, human environment, and nature. Weather becomes as important as the artist's design. Large groups of 'initiated' participants and spontaneous sympathizers make a sky event possible, and the 'flying' of this 'flexibly moored balloon' becomes, ideally, a ballet of human motion, wind, and soft sculpture."[1]

[1] From "5 Artists/5 Technologies" catalog, Grand Rapids Art Museum, Grand Rapids, Michigan, 1979.

83

Otto Piene
"Daedalus"
manned helium sculpture
for sky opera, "Icarus"
(Earls, Piene)
"Centerbeam", D.C.
September, 1978
photograph: K.M. Kiely

84

Otto Piene
"Black Rose" and
"Brockton Flower"
sky event for
"Centerbeam", D.C.
photograph: Marc Palumbo

85

Otto Piene

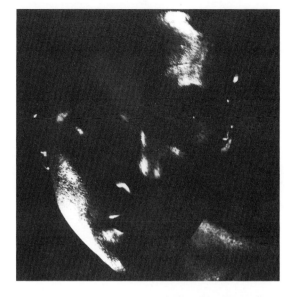

Peter Campus
"Man's Head"
photo projection
"5 Artists/5 Technologies"
Grand Rapids Art Museum
Grand Rapids, Michigan
1979
image by Peter Campus

Otto Piene
"Icarus"
timed inflatable sculpture
"5 Artists/5 Technologies"
Grand Rapids Art Museum
Grand Rapids, Michigan
1979
photograph:
Craig Vander Lende

Otto Piene
"Icarus"
timed inflatable sculpture
"5 Artists/5 Technologies"
Grand Rapids Art Museum
Grand Rapids, Michigan
1979
photograph:
Craig Vander Lende

Technology for Art [1]

The theme which initially inspired the selection of
artists in the exhibition, "Five Artists — Five
Technologies", was LIGHT. The way it was
explained to me by Enid Packard and Janet
Watkins (chairwomen of the Women's Committee)
and Fred Myers (then director of the Grand
Rapids Art Museum) reminded me of the Art and
Technology and LIGHT SHOWS of the 50's and
60's (notably "Bewogen Beweging", Stedelijk
Museum, Amsterdam, 1961; "Kunstlichtkunst",
Stedelijk Van Abbemuseum, Eindhoven, Holland,
1966; "The Machine as Seen at the End of the
Machine Age", Museum of Modern Art, New York
City, 1968-69; "Art and Technology", Los
Angeles County Museum of Art, 1970-71;
"Kinetics", Hayward Gallery, London, 1970).

The Center for Advanced Visual Studies, M.I.T.
contributed its own version of "those" shows—
"Explorations", 1970, at the National Collection
of Fine Arts, Smithsonian Institution. Organized
by Gyorgy Kepes, the founding director of
C.A.V.S., it presented work by C.A.V.S. Fellows
and guests. It was to be the U.S. contribution to
the '69 Sao Paolo Biennale but was never shipped
because of political protest by "47% of the invited
participants"—due to reputation of dictatorship in
Brazil. Gyorgy Kepes started the Center in 1967
and invited (in chronological order) Harold
Tovish, myself, Vassilakis Takis, and Jack Burnham
as a first group of resident kinetic artist/Fellows—
later to be followed by such "technologically
inclined" colleagues as Wen Ying Tsai, Stan
VanDerBeek, and Paul Earls.

Kepes' philosophy—as I take the liberty to abbre-
viate it—involved interpreting and persuasively
disseminating his conviction that responsible
scientists, scholars, engineers, and artists ought to
work together fruitfully in a humanistic spirit for
a better spiritual and physical environment—
especially after the shattering experiences of
World War II. Kepes never tired of pointing out
common goals and uniting intellectual values
among academic equals of different trades. In the
name of humanity and the better world lying
ahead nuclear physicists, sociologists, architect/
planners, engineers, and artists would collaborate
to "realize our dreams".

I feel that the "shared utopia" is related to the
spirit of the United Nations and affiliated organizations—necessary, laudable, "good" and in constant danger of being dominated by strong political
"personalities"—nations of power, wealth
(success!) and individuality which overshadow the
somewhat abstract reasonability of the plenum.
The problem of personality has beset group move-
ments among artists (the Spanish Equipo '57 of
anti-individualist artists never really surfaced, and

Paul Earls
Laser room projections
photograph:
Mennerich/McCann

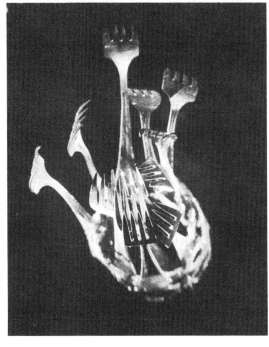

Harriet Casdin-Silver
hologram, "Equivocal
Forks", "Centerbeam"
documenta 6
and Washington, D.C.
1977/78
photograph:
Nishan Bichajian
C.A.V.S./M.I.T.

"giving" could be interpreted as scientists "serving" expression and human imagery rather than mathematical truths or "objective visualization". Any vehicles and media out of technology are good for "the art" only if they further major artistic objectives: image-making, image-processing, or image-distribution. Recent technologies, such as video/TV systems have had considerable influence on image-making (conditioning of images) in view of widespreading distribution techniques. The role of e.g. video synthesizers in image-processing is undeniable—just as the close-to-symbiotic cooperation among "media artists", scientists, and engineers is an obvious example of the "marriage" of complementing opposites.

Academic nomenclature for resident artists at the Center for Advanced Visual Studies at M.I.T. is "research fellows". The research in the arts which makes eminent sense—and must have priority over scientific understanding of research—is the search for new "imagery", i.e. new images, new languages, new vocabulary. The *eidos* reigns above everything in the artist's hierarchy of values.

There are technologies which "enhance" images (even "generate" them?)—such as high-frequency electric-discharge processes or the arsenal of laser techniques and accessories. Techniques can become important determinants in the "total picture" of a work of art—at the outset of "production", "in the middle" (processing), or in the delivery stage (distribution). Without conceiving, perceiving, and guiding artists, or artists' sensitivity, sensibility, spirit, however, they are useless. How, then, is the much-yahooed copulation of artists, scientists, and engineers working at all?

First, scientists and engineers can obviously be implementors for artists—to the degree at which they provide entire "media" and distribution systems as well as image-enhancing devices. Second, they can offer intellectual, spiritual, "scientific" information and know-how; let us also call it "inspiration". Third, they can point at sensually and intellectually perceivable "worlds"—interesting and, sometimes, hitherto unknown to the artists.

If these "aids" mainly support art and artists—what can the latter do for the former? Clearly the situation can be reversed, with limits: As the scientist cannot do the artist's art, the artist cannot do the scientist's science but he can serve science—in the name of science—by providing an extra eye, ear, "sense", "vision", method of intuition, formulation of language—besides "design services", "experience by application" and other clarifying practice. In contrast to Gyorgy Kepes, I began pointing out differences rather than commonness among artists and scientists ("art and technology") soon after I assumed responsibility for C.A.V.S.

the "nameless" Italian gruppo n of Padua vanished a few years after its formation). My contrasting position became manifest with Group Zero of Düsseldorf (formed 1957), in which artist individuals with names volunteered to share goals and activities in typical democratic fashion. However, the strong personalities involved veered apart after nine successful years of grouped common as well as grouped individual artistic life and work.

Not only does collaboration among artists, scientists, and engineers have to live with personality ("ego") problems but, on a larger scale, so does the integration of efforts out of the fields of art, science, engineering (business, I should add—and government). Works of art—environmental or not—are by definition highly individual, highly personal statements. The subjectivity of artistic statements—whether creative or merely judgemental—is in direct contrast to the, by definition, desirable objectivity of science and technology. In the mating of contributions personalities and articulated energies can blend only if "something gives". If the intended results are "art", then integration will have to happen in the name of art. The

Otto Piene
"Grand Rapids Carousel"
for Festival '79
Calder Plaza
Grand Rapids, Michigan
June, 1979
photograph:
Craig Vander Lende

If "that marriage" is to make sense it will "unite" polar disparities and make them work for "art"— which may then inspire a growing audience (as we all hope)—or "for science" (but hardly for something "greater than both" yet). (Leonardo designed flying machines but did not fly.)

Albrecht Dürer may have had visions of nuclear holocaust but he did not build the atom bomb. The atom bomb along with many other products of "scientific objectivity" and resulting engineering was built by scientists and engineers. The artistic commitment to imagery confines the artist to the freedom of play—visual, musical, "environmental". Play is often spiritually serious but "practically" frivolous—whereas "reality" including much scientific and engineering reality—is often practically serious but spiritually frivolous and invoking fatal danger. Art does not kill—but for better or worse— its healing capacity is less measurable than surgery and medically applied radiation.

Artists used to lead vision during historic periods of religious guidance. Where is the artist in this time when praying for enlightenment has been replaced by research? I think that minds, methods, and practice will come together again in a more binding, challenging manner when the new TIME will appear and we shall move and work in space. Utopia again? New forms of existence, insight, and communication will develop only if all creative capacity of soul and mind may constitute new forms of what? Science fiction? Art fiction? A new fiction called reality?

What can be gained for art for the time being? Technology facilitates a large scale for objects and events of art. Technology facilitates an enormous scale of distribution, communication, and expansion. Technology implements expression of: movement in time; appearance in space; travel of energies; and change of humans. However, technology is many things to many interests. What Kepes really wants is technology to be persons who care and "art" to be artists who face the provocation and meet the challenge and scale of technology (science, engineering, etc., etc.).

Of the standard magic words in recent "kinetic" language—video, computer, laser, hologram—only two are quoted in full in this exhibition (Paul Earls' laser piece; Harriet Casdin-Silver's holograms); "computer" is only present as a programming device for the laser scanners, and Peter Campus' image projection marks his "next step" toward intensified (human) imagery beyond existing video tools. My inflatables and sky events, "Carousel" (of human images), attempt to point at the new dimension of nature, life, science, and art: SKY—and so does Alejandro Sina's sophisticated play with light and lightning. The Five Technologies are vehicles permitting intensified

expressions in time and space of the Five Artists' varied work. Besides LIGHT, their unifying concerns appear to be the human image and the space in which it flies.

[1] Reprinted by generous permission of the Grand Rapids Art Museum; the essay was written for "5 Artists/ 5 Technologies — Environmental Lightworks by Peter Campus, Harriet Casdin-Silver, Paul Earls, Otto Piene, Alejandro Sina", an exhibition and three sky events of the Grand Rapids Art Museum, May 24 through July 15, 1979.

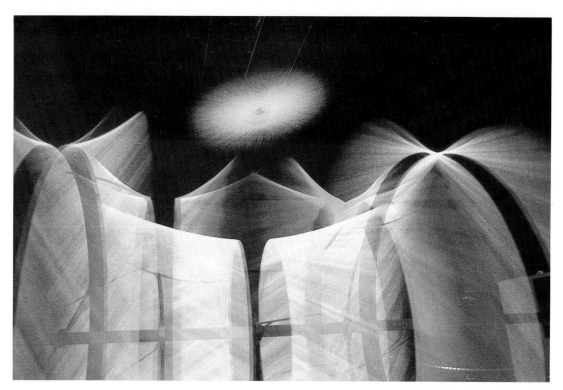

Alejandro Sina
Installation of moving
neon sculptures
"5 Artists/5 Technologies"
Grand Rapids Art Museum
Grand Rapids, Michigan
1979
photograph: Ed Saunders

Fellows, C.A.V.S.
(January, 1980)

Mitchell Benoff
Nishan Bichajian
Joan Brigham
Mira Cantor
Harriet Casdin-Silver
Betsy Connors
Chryssa
Paul Earls
Wendelin Glatzel
Elizabeth Goldring
George Greenamyer
Christopher Janney
Piotr Kowalski
Ellen Kozak
Mandi McIntyre
Mark Mendel
Mit Mitropoulos
Antonio Muntadas
Michael Naimark
Carl Nesjar
Yvonne Rainer
Aldo Tambellini
Donald Thornton

Mira Cantor
"Elevator", 1976
life-scale soft sculpture
canvas, oil, accessories
photograph:
Nishan Bichajian
C.A.V.S./M.I.T.

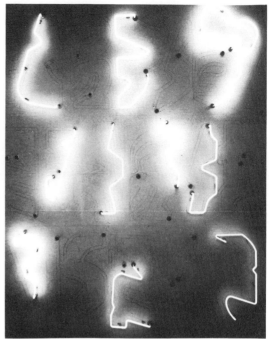

Chryssa
"That's All"
1971
9' x 8', neon and plexiglass
collection: Metropolitan
Museum of Art, New York
New York
photograph:
Henry Gronskinsky

Piotr Kowalski
"The Mirror", 1979
four double-sided mirrors
each 72"x173¼" on
motorized revolving base
photograph: eeva-inkeri
Feldman Fine Arts
New York City

Yvonne Rainer
still image from
"Journeys from Berlin
1971"
Yvonne Rainer image

Past Fellows
(partial list,
January, 1980)

Maryanne Amacher
Karin Bacon
Juan Navarro Baldeweg
Mauricio Bueno
Lowry Burgess
Peter Campus
Muriel Cooper
Dan Dailey
Douglas Davis
Juan Downey
Charles R. Frazier
Elon Goitein
John Goodyear
Virginia Gunter
Ron Hays
Michio Ihara
Toshiro Itakura
Rockne Krebs
Paul Matisse
Miralda
Mike Moser
Avatar Da Silva Moraes
John Avery Newman
Alejandro Otero
Gary Thomas Rieveschl
Jon Rubin
Friedrich St. Florian
Alejandro Sina
Alan Sonfist
Peter Struycken
Vassilakis Takis
Harold Tovish
Wen-Ying Tsai
Stan VanDerBeek
Howard Alan York

Charles Frazier
from "Gas"
a happening with
Alan Kaprow
Southampton, New York
summer, 1966

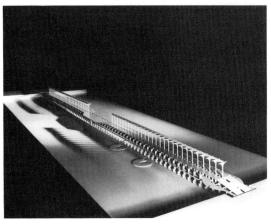

Friederich St. Florian
Model for new Harvard
Bridge
Charles River Project
photograph:
Nishan Bichajian
C.A.V.S./M.I.T.

Wen Ying Tsai
Cybernetic Sculpture
photograph:
Nishan Bichajian
C.A.V.S./M.I.T.

Fellows Meeting
C.A.V.S./M.I.T., 1977
(around the table clockwise
beginning second from left)
O. Piene, A. Hiemer, H.
Casdin-Silver, E. Goldring,
L. Burgess, J. Brigham, K.
Kantor, A. Sina, M. Chow,
K. Bacon, N. Doll, W.
Ahrens, M. Moser, P. Earls,
B. Cadogan, M. Mendel
photograph:
Nishan Bichajian
C.A.V.S./M.I.T.

Lowry Burgess (right)
Nam June Paik (left)
at *documenta* site
Kassel, Germany, 1977
photograph: Dietmar Loehrl

"Centerbeam", D.C.
(left to right) B. Cadogan,
A. McSweeney, O. Piene
photograph:
Elizabeth Goldring

(left to right)
Harriet Casdin-Silver,
Otto Piene, Lowry Burgess
(with mask)
photograph:
Elizabeth Goldring

"Centerbeam" Artists, *documenta 6*

Joan Brigham
Lowry Burgess
Harriet Casdin-Silver
Paul Earls
Elizabeth Goldring
Michio Ihara
Harel Kedem
Gyorgy Kepes
Michael Moser
Carl Nesjar
Otto Piene
Alejandro Sina
Aldo Tambellini

"Centerbeam" Artists, Washington, D.C.

Joan Brigham
Lowry Burgess
Harriet Casdin-Silver
Mark Chow
Betsy Connors
Alva Couch
Paul Earls
Derith Glover
Elizabeth Goldring
Christopher Janney
Gyorgy Kepes
Paul Matisse
Mark Mendel
Michael Moser
Muntadas
Otto Piene
Alejandro Sina
Aldo Tambellini
Don Thornton

Joan Brigham,
Elizabeth Goldring
photograph: Otto Piene

inflatables workshop
navy yard
Washington, D.C.
photograph: Marc Palumbo

Vienna Biennale

Participants
Otto Piene
Harriet Casdin-Silver
Elizabeth Goldring
Paul Earls

Documentation
Lowry Burgess
Paul Matisse
Mira Cantor
Gyorgy Kepes
Miralda
Muntadas
Mark Mendel
Michael Naimark
Aldo Tambellini
Yvonne Rainer
Jon Rubin
Jose Maria Yturralde
Vassilakis Takis

Biographies

Werner Ahrens
photograph: anonymous

Edward Allen
photograph: anonymous

Werner Ahrens
Artist

Born
Oberhausen, Germany, 1948

Education
Studied sculpture with S. Tajiri, Kunsthochschule, Berlin, Germany, 1968-69
Meisterschüler, Kunsthochschule, Berlin, Germany, 1969-74

Appointments
Assistant, Kunsthochschule, Berlin, 1974-76
Research Affiliate, Center for Advanced Visual Studies, Massachusetts Institute of Technology, 1977

Awards and Honors
Airlift Memorial Fellowship, 1976

Contribution to "Centerbeam"
Technical assistance

Edward Blair Allen
Architect

Born
Minneapolis, Minnesota, 1938

Education
University of Wisconsin, Madison, Wisconsin, 1956-58
University of Minnesota, Minneapolis, Minnesota, B. Arch., 1958-62
University of California, Berkeley, California, M. Arch., 1962-64
Università di Roma, Facoltà di Architettura, Rome, Italy, 1966-67

Appointments
Associate, MLTW Architects, Berkeley, California, 1964-66
Fulbright Scholar, Italy, 1966-67
Research Associate, Massachusetts Institute of Technology, Cambridge, Massachusetts, 1968
Assistant Professor, M.I.T., 1968-72
Associate Professor, M.I.T., 1972-
Partner, Allen & Mahone, Architects, Watertown, Massachusetts, 1978-

Special Projects
Stone houses in southern Italy, 1966-67
Ground facilities for a VTOL intercity transportation network, 1968-70
Automated system for the extrusion of building shells, 1969-71
Coated foam housebuilding systems, 1971-73
Private architectural commissions, 1973-

Publications
Lightweight Structures (editor), University of California Press, Berkeley, California, 1963
Stone Shelters, M.I.T. Press, Cambridge, Massachusetts, 1969
The Responsive House (editor), M.I.T. Press, Cambridge, Massachusetts, 1974
How Buildings Work, Oxford University Press, New York, New York, 1979
Teach Yourself to Build, M.I.T. Press, Cambridge, Massachusetts, 1979

Contribution to "Centerbeam"
Consultant on structural design

Stephen Benton
photograph: anonymous

Stephen Benton

Physicist, photographer, holographer

Born

San Francisco, California, 1941

Education

Massachusetts Institute of Technology, Cambridge, Massachusetts, B.S., 1959-63
Harvard University, Cambridge, Massachusetts, Ph.D., 1963-68

Appointments

Assistant Professor of Applied Optics, Harvard University, Cambridge, Massachusetts, 1968-73
Senior Scientist, Research Laboratories, Polaroid Corporation, Cambridge, Massachusetts, 1961-

Awards and Honors

(partial list)
President, Optical Society, New England Section
Consultant to the Holographic Arts Program, Smithsonian Institution
Visiting Committee, International Museum of Photography, George Eastman House
Director, Optical Society of America
Member, International Commission for Optics

Group Exhibitions

"Light and Lens", in collaboration with Harriet Casdin-Silver, Hudson River Museum, Yonkers, New York, 1973
"Light and Substance", in collaboration with Harriet Casdin-Silver, University of New Mexico, Albuquerque, New Mexico, 1975
"Holography 1975: The First Decade", in collaboration with Harriet Casdin-Silver, International Center of Photography, New York, New York, 1975
Seibu Museum of Art, Tokyo, Japan, 1976
Museum of Holography, New York, New York, 1976, 1978
The Mike Douglas Show, 1977
The Tomorrow Show with Tom Snyder, 1977
Gallery 1134, Chicago, Illinois, 1977
Bell Gallery, Rhode Island School of Design, Providence, Rhode Island, 1977
Isetan Art Hall, Tokyo, Japan, 1978

Patents

U.S. patent 3,633,989: Method for making reduced bandwidth holograms, 1972
U.S. patent 3,657,981: Direct orthoscopic stereo panoramagram camera, 1972
U.S. patent 3,944,322: Light filtering arrangement for holographic displays, 1976

Contribution to "Centerbeam"

Consultant

Joan Brigham
photograph:
Francene Keery

Joan Brigham

Environmental sculptor, working with steam as a sculptural medium

Born

Tulsa, Oklahoma, 1935

Education

Pomona College, Claremont, California, B.A., 1952-56
Harvard University, Cambridge, Massachusetts, M.S., 1965

Appointments

Curriculum Planner and Instructor, First Level Program, Emerson College, Boston, Massachusetts, 1971-74
Director, Emerson Internship Program in the Arts, Emerson College, 1973-74
Instructor, Environmental Art, Massachusetts College of Art, Boston, Massachusetts, 1976-
Assistant Professor of Fine Arts, Emerson College, 1976-
Fellow, Center for Advanced Visual Studies, Massachusetts Institute of Technology, Cambridge, Massachusetts, 1974-

One-Person Exhibitions

"Steam Fountains: A proposal for Boston 200", Center for Advanced Visual Studies, Cambridge, Massachusetts, 1975
"Works in Steam: C.A.V.S. Artist Joan Brigham", M.I.T. Lincoln Laboratory, Lexington, Massachusetts, 1977

Events

"Fog, Mist and Dreams", steam and computer-generated graphics, ARTTRANSITION, C.A.V.S./M.I.T., Cambridge, Massachusetts, with Stan VanDerBeek, 1975
"Environmental Music", steam and laser, Center for Advanced Visual Studies, M.I.T., Cambridge, Massachusetts, with Paul Earls, 1975
"Under Aquarius", steam, lights and film projections, M.I.T., Cambridge, Massachusetts, with Stan VanDerBeek, 1976

Joan Brigham
"Steam Screens"
event with steam and film
projections, with
Stan VanDerBeek
Whitney Museum of
American Art
New York, New York
1979
photograph:
Francene Keery

Lowry Burgess
photograph: Phil Bingham

"Dream Screen", Emerson College, Boston,
  Massachusetts, 1976
"Under Aquarius", repeat performance,
  Hampshire College, Amherst, Massachusetts,
  with Stan VanDerBeek and the American
  Underwater Band, 1977, 1978
"Day Work–Night Dreams", Avant-Garde Festival,
  New York City, 1977
"Golem" Steam Theater, Student Union Plaza,
  M.I.T., Cambridge, Massachusetts, with Mark
  Ross, 1978
Conservatoire National des Arts et Métiers, Paris,
  France, 1979

Publications

"Participatory Air Art with Steam as Medium:
  Steam Works", *Leonardo,* Boulogne sur Seine,
  France, Fall issue, 1977

Contribution to "Centerbeam"

Steam line
Water line

Lowry Burgess
Environmental artist

Born
Philadelphia, Pennsylvania, 1940

Education
Pennsylvania Academy of Fine Arts; University
  of Pennsylvania, Philadelphia, Pennsylvania,
  Graduate degree, 1956-61
Institute Allende San Miguel, Mexico, 1959

Appointments
Professor of Visual Fundamentals; Chairman,
  Graduate MFA Program, Massachusetts
  College of Art, Boston, Massachusetts, 1969-
Fellow, Center for Advanced Visual Studies,
  Massachusetts Institute of Technology,
  Cambridge, Massachusetts, 1972-78

Awards and Honors
National Humanities Faculty, 1969-
National Institute of Arts and Letters, 1972
Guggenheim Foundation Grant, 1974-75
National Endowment Individual Artist Grant,
  1977-78
Rockefeller Foundation Artist Grant, 1979

One-Person Exhibitions
(partial list)
"Drawing Cycles and Series", Institute of
  Contemporary Art, Boston, Massachusetts,
  1971
Lamont Library, Fogg Art Museum, Harvard
  University, Cambridge, Massachusetts, 1972
"Lowry Burgess: Drawings", Center for
  Advanced Visual Studies, M.I.T., Cambridge,
  Massachusetts, 1975
Carpenter Center, Harvard University, Cambridge,
  Massachusetts, 1975

Group Exhibitions
(partial list)
"Elements", Boston Museum of Fine Arts,
  Boston, Massachusetts, 1971
Multiple Interaction Team, Center for Advanced
  Visual Studies, M.I.T., Cambridge, Massachu-
  setts, 1972-74

Lowry Burgess
"Listening for Light Hinge"
Charles River
Boston, Massachusetts
1971
photograph: George Cope

Bill Cadogan
photograph: anonymous

CAYAC, Traveling exhibition through Latin
America, 1972-74
ARTTRANSITION, C.A.V.S./M.I.T., Cambridge,
Massachusetts, 1975
"You Are Here", C.A.V.S./M.I.T., Institute of
Contemporary Art, Boston, Massachusetts, 1976
International Biennial Exhibition of Graphic and
Visual Art (C.A.V.S./M.I.T., documentation
room), Vienna, Austria, 1979

Events/Major Works

"Resounding Space", Boston, Massachusetts,
1972
"Charles River Master Plan", Cambridge and
Boston, Massachusetts, 1972-74
"Star-Pits-Waiting-for-Light-Planes", Cincinnati,
Ohio, 1973
"Inclined Galactic Light Pond", Bamiyan,
Afghanistan, 1974
Post Office Square Park, Boston, Massachusetts,
1975-76
"Garden into Air: Utopic Vessel", Easter Island,
South Pacific, 1978
"Quiet Axis, Part II: Utopic Vessel", Rapa Nui
(Easter Island), South Pacific, 1978-79
"Quiet Axis, Part III: Garden into Ether",
Outer Space, 1979-80

Publications

Fragments, 1970; *Looking and Listening,* 1972;
Memory, Environment and Utopia, 1974-75,
Workshop for Learning Things, Boston,
Massachusetts
Programs of Promise, Harcourt, Brace,
Jovanovich, 1974

Contribution to "Centerbeam"

"Centerbeam" idea; artistic director for the
project

William Cadogan
Engineer in a variety of artistic media

Born
Cambridge, Massachusetts, 1947

Education
Massachusetts Institute of Technology, Cambridge,
Massachusetts, B.S. in Electrical Engineering,
1965-69

Appointments
Fellow, Center for Advanced Visual Studies,
M.I.T., Cambridge, Massachusetts, 1978

Events/Major Works
"Sunburst", Worcester Center, Worcester,
Massachusetts, for Otto Piene, 1971
"4th of July Salute", Prudential Center, Boston,
Massachusetts, for Center for Advanced Visual
Studies, M.I.T., 1975
"Anemones", New York, New York, for Otto
Piene, 1976
"Firefly", outdoor light sculpture, Boston,
Massachusetts, 1976
"Golem", Cambridge River Festival, Cambridge,
Massachusetts, for Joan Brigham, 1978
"Art in the Environment", Arcosanti Festival,
Cordes Junction, Arizona, for Otto Piene,
1978
"First Night", Boston, Massachusetts, for Otto
Piene, 1978
"Mermaid", Miami Beach, Florida, for Roy
Lichtenstein, 1979
"Sonia Henie Fountain", Lake Placid, New
York, for Carl Nesjar, 1979

Contribution to "Centerbeam"
Project engineer

(above)
Harriet Casdin-Silver
photograph: John Foraste
Brown University News
Bureau

(above right)
Harriet Casdin-Silver
"Holos # 17", 1973
transmission hologram
photograph: John Foraste
Brown University News
Bureau

Harriet Casdin-Silver

Artist, holographer, designer, lecturer; exploring holographic movies

Born

Worcester, Massachusetts, 1935

Education

University of Vermont, Burlington, Vermont, B.A., 1952-56
New School for Social Research, Columbia University, New York, New York, 1956-58
Cambridge-Goddard Graduate School for Social Change, Cambridge, Massachusetts, 1974

Appointments

Lecturer, Clark University, Worcester, Massachusetts, 1969-74
Artist-in-Residence, American Optical Research Laboratory, Framingham, Massachusetts, 1969-73
Assistant Professor (Research) of Physics, Brown University, Providence, Rhode Island, 1974-78
Fellow, Center for Advanced Visual Studies, Massachusetts Institute of Technology, Cambridge, Massachusetts, 1976-

Awards and Honors

(partial list)
National Endowment for the Arts, 1975
Council for the Arts, M.I.T., 1978
Rockefeller Foundation Fellowship, 1978, 1979

One-Person Exhibitions

(partial list)
"Light-Sound Environments", Clark University, Worcester, Massachusetts, 1969
"Aesthetic Holography", Polaroid Corporation, Cambridge, Massachusetts, 1972
"Harriet Casdin-Silver Holography", Museum of Holography, New York, New York, 1977

Group Exhibitions

(partial list)
Museum of Contemporary Art, Chicago, Illinois, traveling, 1970-71

"Women Choose Women", New York Cultural Center, New York, New York, 1973
International Center for Photography, New York, New York, 1975
ARTTRANSITION, C.A.V.S./M.I.T., Cambridge, Massachusetts, 1975
"Holography", House of Culture, Stockholm, Sweden, 1976
"Holography", Seibu Museum, Tokyo, Japan, 1976
Asahi Shimbun Holography Exhibition, Isetan Museum, Tokyo, Japan, 1978
"5 Artists/5 Technologies", Grand Rapids Art Museum, Grand Rapids, Michigan, 1979
International Biennial Exhibition of Graphic and Visual Art, C.A.V.S./M.I.T., Vienna, Austria, 1979
Franklin Institute, Philadelphia, Pennsylvania, 1979
"Critics' Choice", Liverpool, England, 1979

Events/Major Works

"Exhaust", performance by artist within 10-foot stainless steel cube, E.A.T. Exhibition, Brooklyn Museum, New York, New York, 1968
Originated concept of using laser light alone to compose holographic imagery, 1970
First holographic art of defined substantial frontal projection, 1972
First white-light transmission "art hologram", with Dr. S. Benton, 1972
"Picture This", Museum of Modern Art, New York, New York, 1977
Originated solar-tracked holograms, the first outdoor holographic installation, for "Centerbeam", 1977-78
"A Woman", new holographic format for Grand Rapids Museum and Vienna Biennale, 1979

Public Lectures

(partial list)
Brown University, Providence, Rhode Island, 1976
The Art Institute of Chicago, Chicago, Illinois, 1978
Pennsylvania State University, University Park, Pennsylvania, 1978
Radcliffe College, Cambridge, Massachusetts, 1978
The Smithsonian Institution, Washington, D.C., 1978
Grand Rapids Art Museum, Grand Rapids, Michigan, 1979

Public Collections

Museum of Holography, New York, New York

Contribution to "Centerbeam"

Holography line, holograms and solar tracking units

(right)
Mark Chow
photograph:
Nishan Bichajian
C.A.V.S./M.I.T.

(far right)
Betsy Connors
photograph: self portrait

Mark Chow
Film and video artist

Born
Madison, Wisconsin, 1953

Education
Massachusetts Institute of Technology, Cambridge, Massachusetts, S.B. in Electrical Engineering, 1970-74
Massachusetts Institute of Technology, Cambridge, Massachusetts, S.B. in Architecture, 1974-75

Appointments
Fellow, Center for Advanced Visual Studies, M.I.T., Cambridge, Massachusetts, 1977-79

Contribution to "Centerbeam"
Video

Betsy Connors
Video artist

Born
Cambridge, Massachusetts, 1950

Education
University of Massachusetts, Amherst and Boston, Massachusetts, B.A., 1968-73
Ecole des Beaux Arts and Ecole du Louvre, Paris, France, 1972-73

Appointments
WGBH New Television Workshop Artist, Boston, Massachusetts, 1976-
Member, Board of Directors, Boston Film and Video Foundation, Boston, Massachusetts, 1977-
Research Affiliate, Center for Advanced Visual Studies, M.I.T., Cambridge, Massachusetts, 1977-78, 1980

Awards and Honors
Artist's Fellowship in Video, Massachusetts Arts and Humanities Foundation, 1976
Artist-in-Residence, The Artists Foundation, Boston, Massachusetts, 1978-79

One-Person Exhibitions
Boston Film and Video Foundation, Boston, Massachusetts, 1979

Group Exhibitions
Boston Film and Video Foundation, Boston, Massachusetts, 1976, 1977, 1978
"Filmwomen of Boston", Off the Wall, Cambridge, Massachusetts, 1977
Artists TV Lab Invitational Video Expo '77, Rhinebeck, New York, 1977
B.O.S. Gallery, Boston, Massachusetts, 1977
Addison Gallery of American Art, Andover, Massachusetts, 1978
"Summer Nights", New England Traveling Exhibit, Massachusetts College of Art, Boston, Massachusetts, 1979

Events/Major Works
"Batteries Not Included", WGBH-TV, Boston, Massachusetts, 1979

Contribution to "Centerbeam"
Video

(right)
Alva Couch
photograph: self portrait

(far right)
Paul Earls
photograph:
Nishan Bichajian
C.A.V.S./M.I.T.

Alva L. Couch
Bassoonist, computer programmer

Born
Winston-Salem, North Carolina, 1956

Education
Massachusetts Institute of Technology, Cambridge, Massachusetts, B.S., 1974-78

Appointments
Computer programmer, electron probe analysis, Harvard Medical School, Boston, Massachusetts, 1978-

Contribution to "Centerbeam"
Developmental computer work on laser imagery (D.C.)

Paul Earls
Composer, media artist

Born
Springfield, Missouri, 1934

Education
Eastman School of Music, Rochester, New York, B.M., 1953-55
University of Rochester, Rochester, New York, M.M. and Ph.D. in Composition-Musicology, 1955-59

Appointments
Director of Music, Chabot College, San Leandro, California, 1961-62
Assistant Professor of Music, University of Oregon, Eugene, Oregon, 1962-65
Associate Professor of Music, Duke University, Durham, North Carolina, 1965-72
Visiting Associate Professor of Humanities, M.I.T., Cambridge, Massachusetts, 1971-73
Lecturer, Massachusetts College of Art, Boston, Massachusetts, 1972-
Composer-in-residence; Adjunct Professor, University of Lowell, Lowell, Massachusetts, 1976-77
Lecturer, Department of Architecture, M.I.T., Cambridge, Massachusetts, 1979-80
Fellow, Center for Advanced Visual Studies, M.I.T., Cambridge, Massachusetts, 1970-

Awards and Honors
(partial list)
Benjamin Prize, 1958
Advanced Research Fulbright Fellowship, 1964-65
Guggenheim Fellowship, 1970
National Endowment for the Arts Grants, 1974, 1977

One-Person Exhibitions/Performances
Chamber works, Gardner Museum, Boston, Massachusetts, 1974
"Sounding Space", Hayden Gallery, M.I.T., Cambridge, Massachusetts, 1972

Paul Earls
two scenes from
"Bremen Town Musicians"
one of two chamber operas
("A Grimm Duo", 1977)
costumes: Otto Piene and
Mira Cantor
laser image: Otto Piene
and Alva Couch
photograph:
Nishan Bichajian
C.A.V.S./M.I.T.

Group Exhibitions/Performances

(partial list)

"Composer's Forum Invitational Concert", New
York, New York, 1967

"Dialogue for the Senses", Wadsworth Atheneum
Tactile Gallery, Hartford, Connecticut, 1972

"Weather", C.A.V.S./M.I.T., Cambridge, Massachusetts, 1974

"Food Show", C.A.V.S./M.I.T., Cambridge, Massachusetts, 1975

"Dreamstage: A Multi-Media Portrait of the
Sleeping Brain", Carpenter Center, Harvard
University, Cambridge, Massachusetts, 1977

"5 Artists/5 Technologies", Grand Rapids Art
Museum, Grand Rapids, Michigan, 1979

International Biennial Exhibition of Graphic and
Visual Art, C.A.V.S./M.I.T., Vienna, Austria,
1979

Events/Major Works

(partial list)

"Symposium '70", Duke University, Durham,
North Carolina, 1970

"Who/Ho/Ray", music for film by Stan VanDer-
Beek, 1972

"Flame Orchard", music for sculpture by Gyorgy
Kepes, Bienal Coltejer III, Medellin, Colombia,
1972

"Tent", music for Otto Piene film, 1976

"The Death of King Phillip", opera, Boston,
Massachusetts, 1976

"A Grimm Duo", two operas, Boston and
Cambridge, Massachusetts, 1976-77

"Icarus", sky opera, with Otto Piene, Washington,
D.C., 1978

Commissions

(partial list)

"No Handouts", film, 1968 (awarded 1st Prize,
Atlanta International Film Festival, 1969)

"Ring the Lobby", sound events, M.I.T.,
Cambridge, Massachusetts, 1972

"The Mind's Eye", electronic music and lasers,
Newport Music Festival, Newport, Rhode
Island, 1973

"WERK", music for concert band and computer-
generated tape, Cambridge, Massachusetts, 1973

"The Love Suicide at Schofield Barracks", music
for play, ANTA Theater, New York, New York,
1973

"Music for Oboes and Laser", New York, New
York, 1976; Buffalo, New York, 1977

Recordings/Published Music

"And on the Seventh Day . . . ", Mercury Records,
1958

"Two Wedding Songs", Duke University Press,
Durham, North Carolina, 1972

Choral and organ music published by Ione Press
and Ostara Press

Electronic work published by C.F. Peters

Publications

Articles in *Sound Sculpture,* AEG, Vancouver,
British Columbia, 1975 and *Grove's Dictionary
of Music,* MacMillan, London, England, 1977;
also in *Perspectives of New Music, The
Composer, Yearbook, Inter-American Journal
of Musical Research, Pan Pipes* and *The International Biography of Musicians*

Contribution to "Centerbeam"

Laser line: spectral fan and computer-generated
tapes

Music/sound line

Harold Edgerton
photograph: Steve Grohe

Harold Edgerton

Electrical Engineer
Stroboscopy, ultra-high-speed photography, sonar

Born

Fremont, Nebraska, 1903

Education

University of Nebraska, Lincoln, Nebraska, B.S.,
1925
Massachusetts Institute of Technology, Cambridge,
Massachusetts, S.M. and Ph.D., 1926-31

Appointments

Research Assistant in electrical engineering,
Massachusetts Institute of Technology,
Cambridge, Massachusetts, 1927
Assistant Professor of electrical measurements,
M.I.T., 1932
Associate Professor, M.I.T., 1938
Full Professor, M.I.T., 1948
Institute Professor, M.I.T., 1966
Institute Professor Emeritus, M.I.T., 1968
Instructor, La Fotographia, Venice, Italy, 1979

Awards and Honors

(partial list)
Medal of the Royal Photographic Society of
London, 1936
Modern Pioneers Award, National Association of
Manufacturers, 1940
Potts Medal, Franklin Institute, 1941
Medal of Freedom, 1946
University of Nebraska, Hon. D. Eng., 1948
Joseph A. Sprague Memorial Award, National
Press Photographic Association, 1949
U.S. Camera Achievement Gold Medal Award,
1951
Photography Magazine Award, 1952
Franklin L. Burr Prize, National Geographic
Society, 1953
Progress Medal Award, Photographic Society of
America, 1955
Progress Award, Society of Motion Picture & TV
Engineers, 1959

George W. Harris Achievement Award, Photo-
graphers Association of America, 1959
Gordon Y. Billard Award (outstanding contribu-
tion to students and M.I.T.), 1962
E.I. duPont Gold Medal Award, S.M.P.T.E., 1962
Silver Progress Medal, Royal Photographic Society
of Great Britain, 1964
Morris E. Leeds Award, IEEE, 1965
Technical Achievement Award, A.S.M.E., 1965
Richardson Medal, Optical Society of America,
1968
John Oliver LaGorce Gold Medal, National Geo-
graphic Society, 1968
Doane College (Crete, Nebraska), Hon. LL.D.,
1969
University of South Carolina (Columbia), Hon.
LL.D., 1969
Alan Gordon Memorial Award, S.P.I.E., 1969
Albert A. Michelson Medal, Franklin Institute,
1969
NOGI Award, Underwater Society of America,
1973
Holley Medal (first time jointly awarded —
K. Germeshausen), American Society of
Mechanical Engineers, 1973
National Medal of Science, 1973, awarded by
President Richard Nixon
IEEE Oceanography Coordinating Committee
1974 Award
Member of following societies: Academy of
Applied Science, Academy of Underwater Arts
& Sciences, American Academy of Arts &
Sciences, National Academy of Engineering,
National Academy of Sciences
Fellow of: Institute of Electrical and Electronic
Engineers (IEEE), Photographic Society of
America, Royal Photographic Society of Great
Britain, Society of Motion Picture & TV
Engineers (SMPTE)

One-Person Exhibitions

(partial list)
Compton Gallery, M.I.T., Cambridge, Massachu-
setts, 1978
Vision Gallery, Boston, Massachusetts, 1978

Special Projects

(partial list)
Pioneered research in stroboscopic photography
Perfected the use of stroboscopic lights in both
ultra-high-speed motion and still (stop motion)
photography
Designed watertight cameras with electronic
flash lamps
Consultant on underwater flash photography and
stroboscopy for exploration of sea floors with
Captain Jacques-Yves Cousteau and his
Calypso crew
Developed side-scan sonar technique used to find
the U.S.S. Monitor
Helped to organize and build the New England
Aquarium in Boston

Harold Edgerton image
A tennis serve by
Gussie Moran photographed
at 100 flashes a second

Currently developing sonar devices for positioning equipment in the sea and for exploration of the sub-bottom structure for geological research and underwater archeological exploration

Publications
(partial list)

Moments of Vision: The Stroboscopic Revolution in Photography, with James R. Killian, Jr., The MIT Press, Cambridge, Massachusetts, 1979
Electronic Flash/Strobe, The MIT Press, Cambridge, Massachusetts, 1979

Contribution to "Centerbeam"

Consultant; strobe line (*documenta 6,* Kassel, Germany)

Derith Glover
photograph: Jeffrey Sutton

Derith Glover
Artist involved with the development of a prototypic ocular communications system

Born
Tucson, Arizona, 1952

Education
University of Arizona, Tucson, Arizona, B.F.A., 1970-73
Center for Advanced Visual Studies, Massachusetts Institute of Technology, Cambridge, Massachusetts, S.M.Vis.S., 1975-77

Appointments
Fellow, Center for Advanced Visual Studies, M.I.T., Cambridge, Massachusetts, 1977-78

Group Exhibitions
"Food Show", C.A.V.S./M.I.T., Cambridge, Massachusetts, 1975
"Gas, Glass and Electricity", C.A.V.S./M.I.T., Cambridge, Massachusetts, 1976
"M.S. Thesis Exhibition", Center for Advanced Visual Studies, M.I.T., Cambridge, Massachusetts, 1977
"Collaborative Drawings on Newsprint", with David Covert, M.I.T., Cambridge, Massachusetts, 1977

Projects
"Drawing with Your Eyes", Draper Laboratory/ Center for Advanced Visual Studies, M.I.T., Cambridge, Massachusetts, 1976-77

Contribution to "Centerbeam"
"Drawing with Your Eyes" (D.C.)

Elizabeth Goldring
photograph:
Nishan Bichajian
C.A.V.S./M.I.T.

Elizabeth Goldring

Writer

Born

Forest City, Iowa, 1945

Education

Smith College, Northampton, Massachusetts, B.A.,
    1963-67
Harvard University, Cambridge, Massachusetts,
    M.A., 1974-77

Appointments

Art Department, Missouri Public Schools,
    St. Louis, Missouri, 1969
Field Museum of Natural History, Chicago,
    Illinois (education/exhibits), 1969-70
National Collection of Fine Arts, Smithsonian
    Institution, Washington, D.C. (education),
    1971-72
Children's Museum, Boston, Massachusetts
    (exhibits), 1973-75
Fellow, Center for Advanced Visual Studies,
    M.I.T., Cambridge, Massachusetts, 1975-
Exhibits and Projects Director, Center for
    Advanced Visual Studies, M.I.T., Cambridge,
    Massachusetts, 1978-

Installations and Special Events

Children's Gallery, National Collection of Fine
    Arts, Smithsonian Institution, Washington,
    D.C., 1971-72
Children's Day, National Collection of Fine Arts,
    Smithsonian Institution, Washington, D.C.,
    1971-72
Participative exhibits, Children's Museum, Boston,
    Massachusetts, 1974-75
ARTTRANSITION, Center for Advanced Visual
    Studies, M.I.T., Cambridge, Massachusetts, 1975
"You Are Here", C.A.V.S./M.I.T., Institute of
    Contemporary Art, Boston, Massachusetts, 1976
"5 Artists/5 Technologies", Grand Rapids Art
    Museum (documentation room), Grand Rapids,
    Michigan, 1979
International Biennial Exhibition of Graphic and
    Visual Art (C.A.V.S./M.I.T., documentation
    room), Vienna, Austria, 1979

Publications

You Are Here, M.I.T. and the Institute of Contem-
    porary Art, Boston, Massachusetts, 1976;
    several texts
"Kinetic Sculpture" (editor) for the National
    Endowment for the Arts, 1978
International Biennial Exhibition of Graphic and
    Visual Art, Catalogue, Vienna, Austria, 1979

Contribution to "Centerbeam"

Project Coordinator for both the *documenta 6*
    and Washington, D.C. installations

Michio Ihara
photograph:
Australian Information
Service

Michio Ihara

Sculptor

Born

Paris, France, 1928

Education

Tokyo University of Fine Arts, Tokyo, Japan,
    1949-53

Appointments

Research Associate, Massachusetts Institute of
    Technology, Cambridge, Massachusetts,
    1962-63
Assistant Professor, Musashino Fine Arts Univer-
    sity, Tokyo, Japan, 1966
Fellow, Center for Advanced Visual Studies,
    M.I.T., Cambridge, Massachusetts, 1970-77

Awards and Honors

Graham Foundation Fellowship, 1964
Annual Exhibition Award, American Academy
    and National Institute of Arts and Letters, 1972

One-Person Exhibitions

Kanegis Gallery, Boston, Massachusetts, 1964
Tokyo Gallery, Tokyo, Japan, 1970
Staempfli Gallery, New York, New York, 1977

Group Exhibitions
(partial list)

International Sculptors Symposium, Expo '70,
    Osaka, Japan, 1969
New Zealand International Sculpture Symposium,
    Auckland, New Zealand, 1971
American Academy and National Institute of Arts
    and Letters, New York, New York, 1973
Kyoto and Tokyo Museums of Modern Art, Japan,
    1973-74
"You Are Here", C.A.V.S./M.I.T., Institute of
    Contemporary Art, Boston, Massachusetts, 1976

Commissions
(partial list)

Metal screen, Imperial Theatre, Tokyo, Japan, 1966

Michio Ihara
"Wind Flower", 1976
Model for Long Wharf
Project
"You Are Here"
exhibition (C.A.V.S./
M.I.T.)
Institute of Contemporary
Art
Boston, Massachusetts
photograph:
Nishan Bichajian
C.A.V.S./M.I.T.

Christopher Janney
photograph:
Rochelle Trager

Metal relief, International Christian University,
    Tokyo, Japan, 1967
Metal relief, Fuji Film Company Building, Tokyo,
    Japan, 1969
Sculpture, Monday Plaza, Expo '70, Osaka, Japan,
    1970
Sculpture, Shizouka Press and Broadcasting
    Company Building, Shizouka, Japan, 1970
Sculpture, Wellesley Office Park Building 5,
    Wellesley, Massachusetts, 1973
Sculpture, Civic Plaza, Auckland, New Zealand,
    1975-76
Sculpture, Hyatt Regency Hotel, New Orleans,
    Louisiana, 1976
Sculpture, Central Square, Cambridge, Massachu-
    setts, 1977
Plaza sculpture, Constellation Place, Baltimore,
    Maryland, 1978
Metal screen, Rockefeller Center, New York, New
    York, 1978
Sculpture, Charlestown High School, Boston,
    Massachusetts, 1978
Suspended sculpture, Neiman-Marcus Store,
    Beverly Hills, California, 1979
Suspended sculpture, Saigo Hospital, Kumamoto,
    Japan, 1979

Contribution to "Centerbeam"
Structural design

Christopher Janney
Environmental artist, musician

Born
Washington, D.C, 1950

Education
Princeton University, Princeton, New Jersey, B.A.,
    1969-73
Dalcroze School of Music, New York, New York,
    1975
Center for Advanced Visual Studies, Massachusetts
    Institute of Technology, Cambridge, Massachu-
    setts, S.M.Vis.S., 1976-78

Appointments
Fellow, Center for Advanced Visual Studies,
    M.I.T., Cambridge, Massachusetts, 1978-

Awards and Honors
NEA Grant, "Rooftop Oasis", A Study of Rooftop
    Space in the Urban Environment, Member of
    Haus-Rucker, 1973
Buhl Foundation Grant, "Soundstair on Tour"
    and "Dance for Soundstair", 1979

Group Exhibitions
"Making New York Understandable", Member of
    Haus-Rucker Co., New York Cultural Center,
    New York, New York, 1972
"Wind Harp #1", 13th Annual Avant Garde Art
    Festival, World Trade Center Plaza, New York,
    New York, 1977
"Soundstair", S.M.Vis.S. thesis installation, M.I.T.,
    Cambridge, Massachusetts, 1978
"Soundstair on Tour", Three Rivers Arts Festival,
    Pittsburgh, Pennsylvania, 1979
"Wind-Harp Tunnel", Three Rivers Arts Festival,
    Pittsburgh, Pennsylvania, 1979

Contribution to "Centerbeam"
"Soundshuffle" for "Centerbeam" D.C.

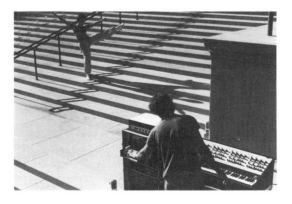

Christopher Janney
"Soundstair on Tour"
(rehearsal, 9/79, with
Dance Collective)
photograph: Anne Bray

(right)
Kenneth Kantor
photograph:
Nishan Bichajian
C.A.V.S./M.I.T.

(far right)
Harel Kedem
photograph:
Nishan Bichajian
C.A.V.S./M.I.T.

Kenneth L. Kantor

Artist, electrical engineer

Born
Downingtown, Pennsylvania, 1956

Education
Massachusetts Institute of Technology, Cambridge, Massachusetts, S.B. in Electrical Engineering, 1975-79

Group Exhibitions
"Food Show", C.A.V.S./M.I.T., Cambridge, Massachusetts, 1975
"Dream Stage: A Multi-Media Portrait of the Sleeping Brain", Carpenter Center, Harvard University, Cambridge, Massachusetts, 1977

Contribution to "Centerbeam"
Electronics for solar tracking of holograms and electronics for sound

Harel Kedem

Artist, architect

Born
Karlsbad, Czechoslovakia, 1947

Education
Painting student of Shimon Kaplan, Rishpon, Israel, 1964-65
Rhode Island School of Design, Providence, Rhode Island, B.F.A., 1972-75; B.Arch., 1975-76
Center for Advanced Visual Studies, Department of Architecture, Massachusetts Institute of Technology, Cambridge, Massachusetts, M.A.A.S., 1976-77

Appointments
Architect, Design Partnership, Boston, Massachusetts, 1977-
Fellow, Center for Advanced Visual Studies, M.I.T., Cambridge, Massachusetts, 1978-79

Awards and Honors
Award in Painting, Tel Aviv Council of the Arts, 1965
Fine Art Award in Painting, Ramat-Gan, Israel, 1968

One-Person Exhibitions
Jewish Community Center, Providence, Rhode Island, 1973
Herter Center, Allston, Massachusetts, 1978
Center for Advanced Visual Studies, M.I.T., Cambridge, Massachusetts, 1978

Group Exhibitions
(partial list)
Z.O.A. House Gallery, Tel Aviv, Israel, 1965
Zvi House Gallery, Ramat-Gan, Israel, 1968
Mishkan-Leomanut, Haifa, Israel, 1971
Traveling exhibition on Russian Jewry, U.S.A., 1974

Professional Activities
Stage design, Galilee Modern Ballet Company, Western Galilee, Israel, 1969
Graphics and prints, Ellat Hotel, Ellat, Israel and Moria Hotel, Jerusalem, Israel, 1970-71
Designed house for Mr. and Mrs. Leibowitz, Galilee, Israel, 1976
Designed the Peles residence and farm in Galilee, Israel, 1979
Monument for the New City Hall, Quincy, Massachusetts, 1979

Contribution to "Centerbeam"
Grow line

Gyorgy Kepes
photograph:
Nishan Bichajian
C.A.V.S./M.I.T.

Gyorgy Kepes
Simulated light play
for Boston Harbor project
1962
photograph:
Nishan Bichajian
C.A.V.S./M.I.T.

Gyorgy Kepes

Painter, photographer, writer and environmental artist; founder and director emeritus of the Center for Advanced Visual Studies

Born

Selyp, Hungary, 1906

Education

Academy of Fine Arts, Budapest, Hungary,
1924-29

Appointments

Head, Light Department, Institute of Design,
Chicago, Illinois, 1937
Professor of Visual Design, Department of
Architecture, M.I.T., Cambridge, Massachu-
setts, 1946-
Visiting Professor, Harvard University, Cambridge,
Massachusetts, 1964-66, 1979
Director, Center for Advanced Visual Studies,
M.I.T., Cambridge, Massachusetts, 1967-74
Institute Professor Emeritus, M.I.T., Cambridge
Massachusetts, 1971-
Artist-in-residence, American Academy in Rome,
Italy, 1974-75

Awards and Honors

(partial list)
Fellow, American Academy of Arts and Sciences,
1952
Rockefeller Foundation Grant, for study on
"The Perceptual Form of the City", Co-
director Kevin Lynch, 1954
Guggenheim Fellowship, 1959-60
Compasso d'Oro, Milan, Italy, 1960
Fine Arts Medal, American Institute of Architects,
1968
Member, National Institute of Arts and Letters,
1968
First Prize, Bienal Coltejer III, Paul Earls and
M. Bueno collaborators, Medellin, Colombia,
1972
Distinguished Bicentennial Professor, University
of Utah, 1975
Andrew W. Mellon Professor, Rice University,
Houston, Texas, 1976

Distinguished Visiting Professor, University of
Cincinnati, Cincinnati, Ohio, 1978
Distinguished Visiting Louis D. Beaumont
Professor of Art, Washington University, St.
Louis, Missouri, 1978
Walker-Ames Professor, University of Washington,
Seattle, Washington, 1978

One-Person Exhibitions

(partial list)
Art Institute of Chicago, Chicago, Illinois, 1944
San Francisco Museum of Art, San Francisco,
California, 1952, 1954
Stedelijk Museum, Amsterdam, Holland, 1955
Baltimore Museum of Art, Baltimore, Maryland,
1959
Hayden Gallery, M.I.T., Cambridge, Massachusetts,
1959
Saidenberg Gallery, New York, New York, 1960,
1963, 1966, 1968, 1970, 1972, 1979
Galerie Moos, Montreal, Canada, 1968, 1974
Boston Museum of Science, retrospective, Boston,
Massachusetts, 1973
State Museum, Mücsarnok, Budapest, Hungary,
and Künstlerhaus, Vienna, Austria, 1976
Bauhaus Museum, Berlin, Germany, 1977
Vision Gallery, Boston, Massachusetts, 1977
Steven Wirta Gallery, San Francisco, California,
1977
Prakapas Gallery, New York, New York, 1977
"The M.I.T. Years: 1945-1977", Hayden Gallery,
M.I.T., Cambridge, Massachusetts, 1978
Henry Gallery, University of Washington, Seattle,
Washington, 1978
Alpha Gallery, Boston, Massachusetts, 1979
Wichita Art Museum, Wichita, Kansas, 1979

Exhibition Design

"Art of the United Nations", Art Institute of
Chicago, Chicago, Illinois, 1944
"Light as a Creative Medium", Carpenter Center,
Harvard University, Cambridge, Massachusetts,
1966; circulated by American Federation of
Arts, 1967
"Explorations", National Collection of Fine Arts,
Smithsonian Institution, Washington, D.C.,
1970

Walter Lewin
photograph: M.I.T.

(above)
Gyorgy Kepes
One of four 130' tall
windows for St. Mary's
Cathedral, San Francisco,
California, 1964-69
P. Belluschi, Luigi Nerri,
A. Mc Sweeney, Architects
photograph: Gyorgy Kepes

(above right)
Gyorgy Kepes
Simulated light effects
floating mirroring buoys
proposal for Bicentennial
Exhibition
Boston Harbor, 1962
photograph:
Nishan Bichajian
C.A.V.S./M.I.T.

Major Works

Kinetic Light Murals, for Radio Shack, Boston, Massachusetts, 1950; for K.L.M., New York, New York, 1960

Glass Windows, St. Mary's Cathedral, San Francisco, California, 1964-65

Publications

(partial list)

The Language of Vision, Paul Theobald & Co., Chicago, Illinois (13 editions), 1944

The New Landscape in Art and Science, Paul Theobald & Co., Chicago, Illinois (4 editions), 1956

Vision and Value series, editor, George Braziller, Inc., New York, New York (7 volumes), 1965, 1966, 1972

"Toward Civic Art", *Leonardo,* Boulogne sur Seine, France, Winter, 1972

Translations of: *Lectures,* Budapest, Hungary, 1978

The Language of Vision, Corvina, Budapest, Hungary, 1978

The New Landscape in Art and Science, Gondôlat, Budapest, Hungary, 1978

A Közossegi müvesietfelé, Magvetö, Budapest, 1978

Public Collections

(partial list)

Hirshhorn Museum, Washington, D.C.
Janos Panonius Museum, Pécs, Hungary
Jerusalem Art Museum, Jerusalem, Israel
Bauhaus Museum, Berlin, Germany

Contribution to "Centerbeam"

Advisor

Walter H.G. Lewin
Nuclear physicist

Born

The Hague, The Netherlands, 1936

Education

University of Delft, The Netherlands, Ir. and Ph.D. in physics, 1954-65

Appointments

Physics Instructor, Libanon Lyceum, Rotterdam, The Netherlands, 1960-66

Staff member, research in experimental nuclear physics, University of Delft, The Netherlands, 1960-66

Assistant Professor of Physics, Massachusetts Institute of Technology, Cambridge, Massachusetts, 1966-68

Associate Professor of Physics, M.I.T., Cambridge, Massachusetts, 1968-74

Professor, M.I.T., Cambridge, Massachusetts, 1974-

Awards and Honors

NASA Award for "Outstanding Scientific Achievement", 1978

Special Projects

Co-Investigator on X-Ray Observations from OSO-7, launched 1971

Co-Investigator on X-Ray Observations from SAS-3, launched 1975

Co-Principal Investigator on High-Energy X-Ray Observations from HEAO-A, launched 1977

Co-Investigator on X-Ray Observations from HEAO-B, launched 1978

Artistic collaboration with Otto Piene since 1967

Artistic collaboration with Peter Struycken since 1978

Publications

About one hundred articles in international journals on astrophysics, physics and astronomy. About ten major review articles in books and journals.

Contribution to "Centerbeam"

Design of solar tracking system

Paul Matisse
photograph:
Peter Jones

Paul Matisse

Inventor, sculptor, machinist

Born
New York, New York, 1933

Education
Harvard University, Cambridge, Massachusetts,
 B.A., 1950-54
Harvard Graduate School of Design, Cambridge,
 Massachusetts, 1954-57

Appointments
Research Associate, State University of New York
 at Albany, 1967-68
Fellow, Center for Advanced Visual Studies,
 Massachusetts Institute of Technology,
 Cambridge, Massachusetts, 1977-79

Group Exhibitions
(partial list)
Institute of Contemporary Art, Boston, Massa-
 chusetts, 1966
Museum of Modern Art, New York, New York,
 1966
Howard Wise Gallery, New York, New York, 1967,
 1968
Milwaukee Art Center, Milwaukee, Wisconsin,
 1968
Krannert Art Museum, Urbana, Illinois, 1969
Musée d'Art Moderne, Paris, France, 1970
Metropolitan Museum of Art, New York, New
 York, 1970
Tel Aviv Museum, Tel Aviv, Israel, 1971
Boston 200, Boston, Massachusetts, 1976
"Aspects of Art and Science", Museum of History
 and Technology, Washington, D.C., 1978;
 Margaret Hutchinson Compton Gallery, M.I.T.,
 Cambridge, Massachusetts, 1979
International Biennial Exhibition of Graphic and
 Visual Art (C.A.V.S./M.I.T., documentation
 room), Vienna, Austria, 1979

Commissions
(partial list)
SUNY at Albany, New York, Atmospheric Science
 Research Center, 1968
Mayo Clinic, Rochester, Minnesota, 1969
Metropolitan Museum of Art, New York, New
 York, 1975
Hayden Planetarium, New York, New York, 1975
Museum of Science, Boston, Massachusetts, 1979

Projects
Developed the Kalliroscope, patented 1967
Kalliroscope Corporation (to design, manufacture,
 and sell various devices showing patterns of
 fluid flow, for aesthetic and/or scientific
 reasons), 1968 to present

Paul Matisse
Kalliroscope, 1979
photograph: Paul Matisse

Executed Alexander Calder's large mobile for the
 National Gallery, Washington, D.C., 1977

Contribution to "Centerbeam"
"Kalliroscopic White River" (D.C.)

113

(right)
Mark Mendel
photograph:
Nishan Bichajian
C.A.V.S./M.I.T.

(far right)
Mark Mendel
Stanza from
"Ojos Numerosos"
Cambridge, Massachusetts
1975
photograph:
Jonathan Newman

Mark Mendel

Poet, environmental artist, stonemason

Born

Monroe, Georgia, 1947

Education

Johns Hopkins University, Baltimore, Maryland,
M.A., 1964-68

Appointments

Instructor, Tuskegee Institute, Alabama, 1968-69
Visiting Poet, Poet-in-the-Schools Program, Maine
State Commission on Arts and Humanities,
1974-80
Visiting Poet, Prison Poetry Workshops, Maine
State Prison/Maine Arts Commission, 1976
Poet-in-residence, Haystack Craft School, Deer Isle,
Maine, 1976
Instructor in Stonemasonry, Haystack at
Arcosanti, Arizona, 1976
Visiting Poet, Georgia Arts Council, 1977
Fellow, Center for Advanced Visual Studies,
Massachusetts Institute of Technology,
Cambridge, Massachusetts, 1976-

Awards and Honors

First Prize, Quality of Life Competition,
Cambridge Arts Council, Cambridge, Massa-
chusetts, 1976
Parklet and Sculpture competition, commission,
"Sunfluent Stonework", Cambridge Arts
Council, Cambridge, Massachusetts, 1979

Readings

Powerhouse Gallery, Montreal, Canada
Auburn University, Albany, Georgia
Princeton University, Princeton, New Jersey
Colby College, Colby, Maine
Renwick Gallery, Washington, D.C.

One-Person Exhibitions

Mississippi Museum of Art, Jackson, Mississippi,
1978
"Stethoscope Laser Inscription", Center for
Advanced Visual Studies, M.I.T., Cambridge,
Massachusetts, 1979

Group Exhibitions

Renwick Gallery, Washington, D.C., 1976
Museum of Contemporary Crafts, New York, New
York, 1977
International Biennial Exhibition of Graphic and
Visual Art (C.A.V.S./M.I.T., documentation
room), Vienna, Austria, 1979
Festa de la Lletra, Barcelona, Spain, 1979

Events/Major Works

Ojos Numerosos, environmental poem, Cambridge,
Massachusetts, 1975
Barn Poem series, rural Maine and Mississippi,
1975-79
Stone/Fire/Place, outdoor fireplaces, Arcosanti,
Arizona, with Paolo Soleri, 1976
Chattahoochee Fast Poem Anthology, children's
environmental poems, Columbus, Georgia,
1977
Cloud Rhymes with Airlines, Boston Kite Festival,
Boston, Massachusetts, 1978

Publications

(partial list)

Poetry published in *New American and Canadian
Poetry,* 1969; *Bellas Artes* (Mexico City), 1970;
Contraband, 1974; *Visible Language, Cold
Spring Journal,* 1975; *North Coast Poetry,
Bartleby's Review,* 1976; *Longhouse, Craft
Horizons, Poets Who Sleep, Poems on Post-
cards,* 1977; *Poetroniques* in *wozu,* Le Soleil
Noir, Paris, 1978; *A Critical Assembling,* New
York City, 1979

Contribution to "Centerbeam"

Poetry line: *Poem On*

114

Charles Miller
photograph: self portrait

Michael Moser
photograph:
Nishan Bichajian
C.A.V.S./M.I.T.

Charles E. Miller
Electrical engineer and computer scientist

Born
Philadelphia, Pennsylvania, 1932

Education
Yale University, New Haven, Connecticut, B.Eng.,
    1957-60
Massachusetts Institute of Technology, Cambridge,
    Massachusetts, S.M., 1961-66

Appointments
Developmental Engineer, General Radio Company,
    1960-72
Lecturer, Electrical Engineering and Computer
    Science Department, M.I.T., Cambridge,
    Massachusetts, 1972-

Projects
(partial list)
Design and construction of portable television
    systems for search and studies of marine life,
    including search at Loch Ness, search for *U.S.
    Monitor, National Geographic* story on lobsters
60 frame/sec. video disc and tape analysis system
    for high-speed videography, studies on up to
    400 frame/sec. system
Design and development of strobes for safety and
    emergency marine applications
Design and construction of high-energy strobes for
    studio and movie photography applications
Design of specialized radar for measurement of
    tennis ball serve velocity
High-speed photography by single-flash, multi-
    flash and high-speed movies

Contribution to "Centerbeam"
Strobe line (not installed)

Michael Moser
Video artist

Born
Baltimore, Maryland, 1952

Education
Clark University, Worcester, Massachusetts, B.A.,
    1970-74
Center for Advanced Visual Studies, Massachusetts
    Institute of Technology, Cambridge, Massachu-
    setts, S.M.Vis.S., 1975-77

Appointments
Fellow, Center for Advanced Visual Studies,
    M.I.T., Cambridge, Massachusetts, 1977-78
Contributing Producer, Maine Public Broadcasting
    Network, 1978-79

Awards and Honors
Artist's Fellowship in Video, Massachusetts Arts
    and Humanities Foundation (The Artists
    Foundation), 1978

One-Person Exhibitions
"The Video Show", School of the Museum of
    Fine Arts, Boston, Massachusetts, 1977
Calliope Gallery, Baltimore, Maryland, 1977

Group Exhibitions
"Food Show", C.A.V.S./M.I.T., Cambridge, Massa-
    chusetts, 1975
ARTTRANSITION, C.A.V.S./M.I.T., Cambridge,
    Massachusetts, 1975
"Art and Technology", Towson College,
    Baltimore, Maryland, 1976
"M.S. Thesis Exhibition", Center for Advanced
    Visual Studies, M.I.T., Cambridge, Massachu-
    setts, 1977
Ithaca Video Festival, traveling exhibition, 1978
Washington, D.C. Video Artists Exhibition,
    Washington Area Film League, 1979

Contribution to "Centerbeam"
Video

Antonio Muntadas
photograph:
Gonzalo Mezza

Muntadas

Media artist

Born
Barcelona, Spain, 1942

Education
University of Barcelona, Spain, 1959-62
Escuela Tecnica Superior Ingenieros Industriales,
    Barcelona, Spain, M.A., 1963-67

Appointments
Fellow, Center for Advanced Visual Studies,
Massachusetts Institute of Technology,
    Cambridge, Massachusetts, 1977-

Awards and Honors
Sumner Foundation for the Arts, 1976, 1978
Fundacion Juan March, Madrid, Spain, 1977

One-Person Exhibitions
(partial list)
Galeria Vandres, Madrid, Spain, 1971-74
Galeria Pecanins, Mexico City, Mexico, 1973
The Video Distribution, New York, New York,
    1975
The Kitchen, New York, New York, 1976
Galeria Ciento, Barcelona, Spain, 1976
Internationaal Cultureel Centrum, Antwerp,
    Belgium, 1976
Everson Museum of Art, Syracuse, New York,
    1977
Anthology Film Archives, New York, New York,
    1978
P.S.I., Queens, New York, 1978
The Museum of Modern Art, New York,
    New York, 1978, 1979
Centre National d'Art et Culture, Georges
    Pompidou (Beaubourg), Paris, France, 1979

Group Exhibitions
(partial list)
Artist's Video Tapes, Paleis voor Schone Kunsten,
    Brussels, Belgium, 1975
Sztuka Video I Socjologiczna, Galeria
    Wspolczesna, Warsaw, Poland, 1975
Recycling, Jerusalem Museum, Jerusalem, Israel,
    1975
IX Biennale de Paris, Paris, France, 1975
"Espace Parle", Galerie Gaetan, Geneva,
    Switzerland, 1977
International Biennial Exhibition of Graphic and
    Visual Art (C.A.V.S./M.I.T., documentation
    room), Vienna, Austria, 1979

Special Projects
(partial list)
"Cadaques Canal Local", Cadaques, Spain, 1974
"Project through Latin America", Argentina,
    Brazil, Venezuela, Mexico, 1975-76

"N/E/S/O/", Venice Biennale, Venice, Italy, 1976
"Barcelona District One", Barcelona, Spain, 1976
"The Last Ten Minutes", (Washington, Kassel,
    Moscow), for *documenta 6,* Kassel, Germany,
    1977
"On Subjectivity", Center for Advanced Visual
    Studies, M.I.T., Cambridge, Massachusetts, 1977
The Pacific Rim Slow Scan Project, Vancouver-
    Cambridge-Cook Islands, 1979

Publications
On Subjectivity, Center for Advanced Visual
    Studies and Visible Language Workshop, M.I.T.,
    Cambridge, Massachusetts, 1978

Contribution to "Centerbeam"
Video (D.C.)

Michael Naimark
photograph:
Nishan Bichajian
C.A.V.S./M.I.T.

Michael Naimark

Video artist, filmmaker, environmental artist

Born

Detroit, Michigan, 1952

Education

University of Michigan, Ann Arbor, Michigan,
  B.S., 1970-74
Center for Advanced Visual Studies, Massachusetts
  Institute of Technology, Cambridge, Massachu-
  setts, S.M.Vis.S., 1977-79

Appointments

Coordinator, Future Worlds Program, University
  of Michigan, Ann Arbor, Michigan, 1972-73
Instructor, Residential College, University of
  Michigan, Ann Arbor, Michigan, 1974-75
Fellow, Center for Advanced Visual Studies,
  M.I.T., Cambridge, Massachusetts, 1979-

One-Person Exhibitions

"Two Works of Environmental Media: Moving
  Movies and Dome Projections", Massachusetts
  Institute of Technology, 1978

Group Exhibitions

Ann Arbor Film Festival, Ann Arbor, Michigan,
  1979
International Biennial Exhibition of Graphic and
  Visual Art (C.A.V.S./M.I.T., documentation
  room), Vienna, Austria, 1979

Video/Film Works

(partial list)
"What Do You Think The Future Will Be Like?",
  1975
"Jogging", "Spiralling Triangles", "Babies on the
  Subway", 1978
"All My Worldly Things", 1979

Special Projects

Research Director, Spectacle Unlimited, an
  environmental art group, Ann Arbor, Michigan,
  1973-74
Lineman, Michigan Cable TV, Ann Arbor,
  Michigan, 1974-75
Producer, first all slide (54,000) optical videodisk,
  Architecture Machine Group, M.I.T., 1978
Filmmaker, Aspen moviemap project for inter-
  active videodisk use, Architecture Machine
  Group, M.I.T., 1978-79

Contribution to "Centerbeam"

Participant, hologram solar-tracking system
Assistant, "Centerbeam" film

Carl Nesjar
photograph: anonymous

Carl Nesjar

Sculptor, photographer

Born

Larvik, Norway, 1920

Education

Pratt Institute, New York, New York, 1936-38
National School of Arts and Crafts, and Royal
  Academy of Art, Oslo, Norway, 1940-42
Columbia University, New York, New York,
  1946-48

Appointments

Guest and Fellow, Center for Advanced Visual
  Studies, M.I.T., Cambridge, Massachusetts,
  1975-

Awards and Honors

French Government Scholarship, 1954-55
Norwegian Endowment Fund, 1971

One-Person Exhibitions

Institute of Contemporary Art, London,
  England, 1967
Hayden Gallery, M.I.T., Cambridge, Massachusetts,
  1975
"Earth, Snow, Ice", University of Chicago,
  Illinois, 1977
"Mud and Ice Photographs", Center for Advanced
  Visual Studies, M.I.T., Cambridge, Massachu-
  setts, 1977

Commissions

(partial list)
Photomurals, World's Fair, Brussels, Belgium,
  1958
Photomurals, tapestries, murals in cut stone, and
  concrete reliefs for buildings in Oslo, Norway
  and Paris, France and for a municipal park in
  Hamburg, Germany

117

Carl Nesjar
"All Year Fountain"
at the Norwegian
Agricultural University
south of Oslo
stainless steel and corten
height 25'
1970
photograph: Carl Nesjar

Murals and sculptures in sand-blasted concrete
("betrograve technique") with Pablo Picasso in
Norway, Sweden, Holland, France, Spain,
Israel and the U.S., including "Figure
Découpée", M.I.T., Cambridge, Massachusetts,
1975
"All-year" or "Ice" fountains at Stabekk and
Oslo, Norway; Moderna Museet, Stockholm,
Sweden; and Flaine, French Alps
Project for small park, with 2 fountains and play
area near Oslo, Norway, 1977
Fountains for new City Hall, Moss, Norway, 1977
Fountain for the Lake Placid 1980 Winter
Olympics, Lake Placid, New York, 1979

Public Collections

National Gallery, Oslo, Norway
Riksgalleriet, Oslo, Norway
Varmlands Museum, Karlstad, Sweden
Gallery of Fine Art, Goteborg, Sweden
Museum of Modern Art, New York City
Moderna Museet, Stockholm, Sweden

Contribution to "Centerbeam"

Brine line

Marc Palumbo
photograph: self portrait

Marc A. Palumbo
Artist

Born
Frankfurt, Germany, 1953

Education
Alderson-Broaddus College, Philippi, West
Virginia, 1971-72
University of Maryland, Baltimore, Maryland,
1972-

Appointments
Fellow, Center for Advanced Visual Studies,
M.I.T., Cambridge, Massachusetts, 1978

Awards and Honors
National Deans List and Scholarship, University
of Maryland, 1979

Special Projects
Formed performance group "The New Wing",
1978
"Dreamstage: A Multi-Media Portrait of the
Sleeping Brain", design and installation for
Paul Earls, Carpenter Center, Harvard Univer-
sity, Cambridge, Massachusetts, 1977
"Poetronics", electronics and execution for Mark
Mendel, Cambridge, Massachusetts, 1978
"Poetronics New Technologies Show", for Mark
Mendel, University of Maryland, 1979
First Night, technical assistance for Otto Piene,
Boston, Massachusetts, 1978
"5 Artists/5 Technologies", technical assistance
for Otto Piene, Paul Earls, Harriet Casdin-
Silver, Alejandro Sina, Peter Campus, Grand
Rapids Art Museum, Grand Rapids, Michigan,
1979
International Biennial Exhibition of Graphic and
Visual Art, C.A.V.S./M.I.T., (technical assistance),
Vienna, Austria, 1979

Contribution to "Centerbeam"
Technical assistance, surveillance, and
maintenance (D.C.)

Otto Piene

Painter, writer, and environmental artist

Born

Laasphe, Westphalia, Germany, 1928

Education

Academy of Fine Arts, Munich, Germany, 1949-50
Academy of Fine Arts, Düsseldorf, Germany,
    1950-52
University of Cologne, Germany, Staatsexamen in
    Philosophy, 1952-57

Appointments

Visiting Professor, Graduate School of Art,
    University of Pennsylvania, Philadelphia,
    Pennsylvania, 1964
Professor for Environmental Art, School of
    Architecture and Planning, Massachusetts
    Institute of Technology, Cambridge, Massachu-
    setts, 1972-
Director, Center for Advanced Visual Studies,
    M.I.T., Cambridge, Massachusetts, 1974-

Awards and Honors

(partial list)

Prize, Deutsche Kunst, Baden-Baden, Germany,
    1959
Grand Prize for Group Zero, IV Biennale Inter-
    nazionale d'Arte, San Marino, 1963
Prize, International Exhibitions of Graphic Art,
    Ljubljana, Yugoslavia, 1967, 1969
Konrad von Soest Prize, Münster, Germany,
    1968
Prize, Ile Exposition International de Dessins
    Originaux, Rijeka, Yugoslavia, 1970
Prize of the National Museum of Modern Art,
    The Eighth International Biennial Exhibition
    of Prints in Tokyo, Japan, 1972
Prize, International Graphics Biennale, Frederik-
    stad, Norway, 1976

One-Person Exhibitions

(partial list)

Galerie Schmela, Düsseldorf, Germany, 1959,
    1960, 1962, 1963, 1966
McRoberts and Tunnard Gallery, London,
    England, 1962, 1964
Howard Wise Gallery, New York, New York,
    1965, 1969, 1970
Museum am Ostwall, Dortmund, Germany,
    retrospective, 1967
Westfälisches Landesmuseum, Münster, Germany,
    1968
Galerie Wendtorf und Swetec, Düsseldorf,
    Germany, 1970, 1972, 1973
Honolulu Academy of Arts, Honolulu, Hawaii,
    1970
Galerie Heseler, Munich, Germany, 1971, 1972,
    1975, 1977, 1978, 1979

(above)
Otto Piene
photograph: Brian Dowley

(below)
Otto Piene
"Milwaukee Anemone"
First Night 1978-79
Boston Common, Boston
Massachusetts
photograph: Paul Foley

Otto Piene
"Olympic Rainbow"
closing ceremony
Munich Olympics, 1972
photograph: Wolf Huber

Kölnischer Kunstverein, Cologne, Germany,
    retrospective, 1973
Hayden Gallery, M.I.T., Cambridge, Massachusetts,
    1975
Galerie Schoeller, Düsseldorf, Germany, 1977,
    1980
Fitchburg Art Museum, Fitchburg, Massachusetts,
    1977
Galerie Heimeshoff, Essen, Germany, 1974, 1977

Group Exhibitions

(partial list)

"Painting and Sculpture of a Decade", Tate
    Gallery, London, England, 1964
"Inner and Outer Space", Moderna Museet,
    Stockholm, Sweden, 1966
"ZERO-Room", Kunstmuseum, Düsseldorf,
    Germany, 1973
"Zero — Bildvorstellungen einer europäischen
    Avantgarde 1958-64", Kunsthaus, Zürich,
    Switzerland, 1979
"Zero", Koninklijk Museum voor Schone Kunsten,
    Antwerp, Belgium, 1979/80
International Biennial Exhibition of Graphic and
    Visual Art, C.A.V.S./M.I.T., Vienna, Austria, 1979
"5 Artists/5 Technologies", Grand Rapids Art
    Museum, Grand Rapids, Michigan, 1979

Events/Major Works

Formed Group Zero with Heinz Mack, 1957
First public performance of "Light Ballet", 1959
"Salon de Lumière" at "nul" exhibition, Stedelijk
    Museum, Amsterdam, Holland, with Heinz
    Mack and Günther Uecker, 1962
"The Fire Flower", multi-media play, Theater
    Diogenes, Berlin, Germany, 1964
"Black Gate Cologne", TV performance, Cologne,
    Germany, with Aldo Tambellini, 1968
"Manned Helium Sculpture" for "Electronic Light
    Ballet", NET-TV, 1969
"Citything Sky Ballet", Pittsburgh, Pennsylvania,
    1970

(above)
Otto Piene
"Light Satellite"
daylight and night star for
Central State Athletic
College
Olympic Area, Munich
Kinetic light, steel, prisms
sculpture
2 strobe lights designed by
Harold Edgerton
frame 100 feet high
with Mitchell Benoff
1971-72
photograph: Wolf Huber

(above right)
Otto Piene
"Lobster Fountain"
model proposal for Long
Wharf, Boston, Massachu-
setts, "You Are Here"
exhibition
Institute of Contemporary
Art
Boston, Massachusetts
1976
photograph:
Nishan Bichajian
C.A.V.S./M.I.T.

(bottom right)
Otto Piene
"Black Stacks Helium
Sculpture"
for "Mississippi"
Walker Art Center
Minneapolis, Minnesota
1975
photograph:
Eric Sutherland/
Walker Art Center

"Charles River Rainbow", Boston/Cambridge,
    Massachusetts, 1971
"Light Satellite", Olympics Communication Center,
    XX. Olympiad, Munich, Germany, 1972
"Olympic Rainbow", closing ceremony of XX.
    Olympiad, Munich, Germany, 1972
"Light Trail", "Tent 2", "Lava Dance", "Flaming
    Rainbow" on Hawaii volcanoes and in Yokohama
    Bay, Oahu, Hawaii, 1974, film for German TV
"Fourth of July Salute", C.A.V.S./M.I.T.,
    Prudential Center, Boston, Massachusetts, 1975
"Neon Rainbow", ARTTRANSITION, C.A.V.S./
    M.I.T., Cambridge, Massachusetts, 1975; and
    Central Park, New York City, 1976, with
    Alejandro Sina
"Anemones: An Air Aquarium", New York,
    New York, 1976
"Milwaukee Anemone", Milwaukee Art Center,
    Milwaukee, Wisconsin, 1977, 1978; and Boston,
    Massachusetts, 1978
"Iowa Star", sky event, Iowa State University,
    Ames, Iowa, 1979
"Grand Rapids Carousel", Grand Rapids Art
    Museum and Arts Festival, Grand Rapids,
    Michigan, 1979
"Iowa Star" and "Grand Rapids Carousel",
    installations and sky event for '79 Vienna
    Biennial Exhibition of Graphic and Visual Art,
    C.A.V.S./M.I.T., Vienna, Austria, 1979

Public Collections
(partial list)

Stedelijk Museum, Amsterdam, Holland
Museum of Contemporary Art, Belgrade, Yugo-
    slavia
Musées Royaux des Beaux Arts, Brussels, Belgium
Kunstmuseum der Stadt, Düsseldorf, Germany
Walker Art Center, Minneapolis, Minnesota
The Museum of Modern Art, New York, New
    York
National Gallery of Canada, Ottawa, Canada
National Museum of Modern Art, Tokyo, Japan
Museum des 20 Jahrhunderts, Vienna, Austria
Nationalgalerie, Berlin, Germany
Kunsthaus, Zürich, Switzerland

Commissions
(partial list)

Light sculptures, City Opera House, Bonn,
    Germany, 1964
Light sculpture, Wormland store facade, Cologne,
    Germany, 1966
"Sun" and "Moon", light sculptures, Hawaii State
    Capital, 1970
Interior and exterior light and elements environ-
    ments, new University of Constance, Germany,
    1970-75
"Sunburst", kinetic light sculpture, Worcester
    Center, Worcester, Massachusetts, 1971
700-foot murals, Rosenthal factory building,
    Selb, Bavaria, 1973

Publications
(partial list)

By the artist:
ZERO magazines 1, 2 and 3, co-published with
    Heinz Mack, 1958-61
More Sky, M.I.T. Press, Cambridge, Massachusetts,
    1973
ZERO, M.I.T. Press, Cambridge, Massachusetts,
    1973
About the artist:
Otto Piene by Jürgen Wissman, Recklinghausen,
    Germany, 1976
Otto Piene by Lawrence Alloway, St. Gallen,
    Switzerland, 1980
Lawrence Alloway, Gyorgy Kepes, Dietrich
    Mahlow et al., "Otto Piene – Werkverzeichnis
    der Druckgraphik", Karlsruhe, Germany, 1977

Contribution to "Centerbeam"

Project director
Two sky events for "Centerbeam", *documenta 6*,
    and twenty-five sky events for "Centerbeam",
    D.C.

Brian Raila
photograph:
Nishan Bichajian
C.A.V.S./M.I.T.

Brian Raila
Film and video artist

Born
Baltimore, Maryland, 1954

Education
Maryland Institute of Art, Baltimore, Maryland,
1972
Massachusetts Institute of Technology, Cambridge,
Massachusetts, S.B. in Art and Design, 1975-77

Appointments
Instructor, University Film Study Center Summer
Institute on Film and Photography, Amherst,
Massachusetts, 1975-77
Instructor, Acting and Television Workshop,
Massachusetts Institute of Technology, 1975-77
Instructor, WGBH New Television Workshop,
WGBH-TV, Boston, Massachusetts, 1974-77

One-Person Exhibitions
"Illusion", Artists Showcase, WGBH-TV, Boston,
Massachusetts, 1977
"Timepiece", Artists Showcase, WGBH-TV,
Boston, Massachusetts, 1978

Group Exhibitions/Screenings
"Food Show", C.A.V.S./M.I.T., Cambridge, Massa-
chusetts, 1975
Center Screen, Boston, Massachusetts, 1976
Off the Wall, Cambridge, Massachusetts, 1977
Institute of Contemporary Art, Boston, Massachu-
setts, 1977
First Night, Boston, Massachusetts, 1977, 1978
Humboldt Film Festival, Arcata, California, 1978
Atlanta Independent Film and Video Festival,
Atlanta, Georgia, 1978
Boston Film and Video Foundation, 1978, 1979

Events/Major Works
(partial list)
"Timepiece", 1976
"Life is a Carnival", 1977
"Miscellus Saccus", 1977
"A la Carte", 1977
"Paper Cycle", 1977
"Loose Leaves", 1978
"Floor Film", 1978
"Fashion Seen", 1978

Contribution to "Centerbeam"
Participant, hologram solar-tracking system

Alejandro Sina
photograph:
Nishan Bichajian
C.A.V.S./M.I.T.

Alejandro Sina
Environmental sculptor, kinetic sculptor

Born
Santiago, Chile, 1945

Education
Universidad de Chile, Santiago, Chile, M.A.,
1971-73

Appointments
Research and teaching technology of materials,
School of Fine Arts, Universidad de Chile,
Santiago, Chile, 1971-72
Fellow, Center for Advanced Visual Studies,
Massachusetts Institute of Technology,
Cambridge, Massachusetts, 1973-1979

Awards and Honors
Fulbright Fellowship, 1973-75
National Endowment for the Arts, 1976-77

One-Person Exhibitions
"Gaslight Phenomena", Institute of Contemporary
Art, Boston, Massachusetts, 1977
"Gaslight Phenomena II", Theo Portnoy Gallery,
New York, New York, 1978

Group Exhibitions
(partial list)
United States-Chilean Institute, 1970, 1971
Museum of Fine Arts, Universidad de Chile,
Santiago, Chile, 1972
Avant-Garde Festival, New York, New York,
1974, 1975
"Boston Celebrations", C.A.V.S./M.I.T., Institute of
Contemporary Art, Boston, Massachusetts, 1975
ARTTRANSITION, C.A.V.S./M.I.T., Cambridge,
Massachusetts, 1975
"You Are Here", C.A.V.S./M.I.T., Institute of
Contemporary Art, Boston, Massachusetts, 1976
"Art and Technology", Towson College, Balti-
more, Maryland, 1976
"Energy Into Art", Memorial Art Gallery,
Rochester, New York, 1978

Alejandro Sina
"Spinning Box #2"
moving neon sculpture
1974-76
photograph:
Nishan Bichajian
C.A.V.S./M.I.T.

"The Expanding Visual World: A Museum of Fun", The Asahi Shimbun Exhibition, Tokyo, Japan, 1979
"5 Artists/5 Technologies", Grand Rapids Art Museum, Grand Rapids, Michigan, 1979

Events/Major Works

"Neon Rainbow", ARTTRANSITION, C.A.V.S./ M.I.T., Cambridge, Massachusetts, 1975; and Central Park, New York, New York, 1976; with Otto Piene
"Neon-Argon Cluster", M.I.T., Cambridge, Massachusetts, 1975

Commissions
(partial list)
Hyatt Regency Hotel, Cambridge, Massachusetts, 1977
Genji Corporation, Boston, Massachusetts, 1977
Landsdowne Corporation, Boston, Massachusetts, 1977
Spalding/Slye Associates, Burlington, Massachusetts, 1977
David Bermant, New York, New York, 1977-78
Broadway Corporation, New York, New York, 1977-79
Hamden Plaza, Hamden, Connecticut, 1979

Public Collections
Museum of Science and Industry, Chicago, Illinois, 1979
The Asahi Shimbun, Tokyo, Japan, 1979

Contribution to "Centerbeam"
Neon-argon line

122

Aldo Tambellini
Filmmaker and media artist

Born
Syracuse, New York, 1930

Education
Art Institute, Lucca, Italy, 1941-46
Syracuse University, Syracuse, New York, B.F.A., 1950-54
Graduate School of Architecture and Allied Arts, University of Oregon, Eugene, Oregon, 1955-56
Notre Dame University, Notre Dame, Indiana, M.F.A., 1957-59

Appointments
Director, Pilot Program in Video, Harlem, New York, 1970-72
Visiting Artist, Art Institute of Chicago, Chicago, Illinois, 1976
Director, Media-Environmental Workshop, School of the Art Institute of Chicago, Illinois, 1977
Fellow, Center for Advanced Visual Studies, M.I.T., Cambridge, Massachusetts, 1976-

Awards and Honors
New York State Council on the Arts, 1969
International Grand Prix, Oberhausen Film Festival, 1969
Experimental TV Lab, NET, New York State Council on the Arts, 1973

One-Person Exhibitions
(partial list)
Museum Wallraf-Richartz, Cologne, Germany, 1968
"Cineprobe", Museum of Modern Art, New York, New York, 1971
"From Film to Video", Anthology Film Archives, New York, New York, 1975
The Media Study Center, Buffalo, New York, 1976
Centerscreen Visiting Artist Series, Carpenter Center, Harvard University, Cambridge, Massachusetts, 1977
The Everson Museum of Art, Syracuse, New York, 1977
"Two-Way Live", Boston Film and Video Foundation, Boston, Massachusetts, 1979

Group Exhibitions
(partial list)
"Television as a Creative Medium", Howard Wise Gallery, New York, New York, 1969
"Black Gate Düsseldorf", (with Otto Piene), Düsseldorf, Germany, 1969
"A Special Video Show", Whitney Museum, New York, New York, 1971
"15 American Video Artists", Centre Culturel Americain, Paris, 1973
"Projekt '74", Kölnischer Kunstverein, Cologne, Germany, 1974

Don Thornton
photograph: Bill Fortune

(above)
Aldo Tambellini
photograph: Ron Marion

(above right)
Aldo Tambellini
"Moonblack"
media event
Carpenter Center
Harvard University
Cambridge, Massachusetts
1977
photograph:
Hans-Christian Lischewsky

ARTTRANSITION, C.A.V.S./M.I.T., Cambridge,
Massachusetts, 1975
"Aesthetics and Technology", The Institute of
Design, Offenbach am Main, Germany, 1978
International Biennial Exhibition of Graphic and
Visual Art (C.A.V.S./M.I.T., documentation
room) Vienna, Austria, 1979

Events/Major Works

Founded first electromedia theater in New York,
New York, 1967
First videotape shown on ABC-TV News, 1967
"Black Gate Cologne", (with Otto Piene), WDR-
TV, Germany, first national television broad-
cast by artists, 1968
"The Medium is the Medium", WGBH-TV, Boston,
Massachusetts, 1969
"The Moving Image Series — Aldo Tambellini:
TV Media Pioneer", WYNE-TV, New York,
New York, 1971
First picturephone two-way live event by artists,
Illinois Bell Telephone, Chicago, Illinois, with
Sonia Sheridan and participants from the
School of the Art Institute of Chicago, 1977

Public Collections

"Black Spiral", TV sculpture, The Everson
Museum of Art, Syracuse, New York
"Black TV", film, Museum of Modern Art, New
York, New York

Contribution to "Centerbeam"

Video

Don Thornton
Painter, sculptor, holographer

Born

Bloomington, Indiana, 1946

Education

Hamilton College, Clinton, New York, B.A., 1964-69
Cooper Union, New York, New York, 1968
Rhode Island School of Design, Providence, Rhode
Island, B.F.A., 1970-74
Villa Schifanoia Graduate School of Art, San
Domenico, Italy, 1973
Center for Advanced Visual Studies, Massachusetts
Institute of Technology, Cambridge, Massachu-
setts, S.M.Vis.S., 1977-79

Appointments

Fellow, Center for Advanced Visual Studies,
M.I.T., Cambridge, Massachusetts, 1979-

One-Person Exhibitions

"Imagine That", thesis exhibition, Center for
Advanced Visual Studies, M.I.T., Cambridge,
Massachusetts, 1979

Group Exhibitions

What Cheer Art Gallery, Providence, Rhode
Island, 1975
"Space Window", Bell Gallery, Brown University,
Providence, Rhode Island, 1977
Cambridge River Festival, Cambridge, Massachu-
setts, 1978
"A Choice of Reality", The Bristol Art Museum,
Bristol, Rhode Island, 1978
"Alice in the Light World", Isetan Museum Holo-
graphy Exhibition, Tokyo, Japan, 1978
"New Spaces", The Franklin Institute, Phila-
delphia, Pennsylvania, 1979

Projects

Research Group: Seeing through opaque barriers
with pico-second laser light pulsed holograms,
Physics Department, Brown University, Providence, Rhode Island, 1979

Contribution to "Centerbeam"

Temporary installation of holograms (D.C.)

Otto Piene
drawing
"Grand Rapids Carousel"
temporary indoor
installation at
Secession, Vienna, Austria
International Biennial
Exhibition of Graphic
and Visual Art
1979

Otto Piene
drawing of
"Wiener Luftspirale"
and "Iowa Star"
laser/inflatables event
with Paul Earls
Secession, Vienna, Austria
International Biennial
Exhibition of Graphic
and Visual Art
1979

124

Concluding Remarks

Holographic images of forks, laser projections drawn on wisps of steam, 23 "sky flower" events, 2 performances of "Icarus" convinced us that we could translate our imagery via these new media into large-scale performances *en plein air.*

Our experiences with "Centerbeam" at *documenta 6* and in Washington, D.C. had the major benefit of bringing imagery and art forms developed in Center studios and M.I.T. laboratories first into the arena of art exhibition and then into the more public arena of public outdoor exhibition. We had learned how to collaborate not only with each other but with the host of technical, environmental and socio-political factors mentioned in preceding texts—essentially how to produce a "road show".

Our next stop—the Vienna International Biennial Exhibition of Graphic and Visual Art (June–July, 1979)—almost inadvertently demonstrated how flexible, spontaneous and adaptable our moveable theatre/circus was becoming. We left many of the stage props behind and pared our hardware shipments to essentials. The performance/events combined inflatable soft sculptures, laser projections and electronic music which had captivated audiences in Kassel and Washington.

Piene's new inflatables were larger than the flowers—the white "Iowa Star"; the 12-figure "Carousel" (his largest figurative sculpture to date) and "Luftspirale" formed of polyethylene tubing. Earls' newly programmed laser projections were more fluidly animated and more closely approached the quality of artistic rendering. We played this palette easily, somewhat confidently.

During indoor performances inflatables became screens for swimming/flying laser projections which freely scanned the entire space—naturally swirling in vortices of light and electronic music.

In Washington, D.C. Piene had wanted to fly "Milwaukee Anemone" and "Black Rose" from the roof of the National Air and Space Museum. In Vienna his "Brockton Flower" emerged from the doors of the Secession (which housed the Biennale exhibition). "Carousel" and "Iowa Star" hovered on the roof offering a day's dialogue with the building's expressive shape, with the Karlsplatz space and Vienna's hazy sky. At night as he flew the "Iowa Star" from the museum parapet, he accomplished what he had planned for the Washington National Air and Space Museum building.

The Star flight was accentuated by laser play on the sculpture, its helium loops, and surrounding trees and buildings—an environmental dance performed to the jabberwocky of urban and street-band tunes.

Prior to Vienna, Center for Advanced Visual Studies artists were commissioned to prepare a portfolio of ideas for large-scale events/performances for the duration of the 1980 Lake Placid Winter Olympics—another "road show" in minus 33° weather?

Since Vienna we have been asked to package and deliver "the show". However, these performances bloom—spectacularly at times—because of the presence of the artists who work *in situ* to produce something that did not exist before. They are revitalized by the process and shared sense of play, spectacle, response and participation—players of contemporary media for an audience of contemporary spectators—modern Icarus and Daedalus for a community of modern gods—everybody.

Elizabeth Goldring
Cambridge, Massachusetts 8/3/79

Otto Piene
"Grand Rapids Carousel"
Festival '79
Calder Plaza, Grand Rapids
Michigan
photograph:
Craig Vander Lende

Otto Piene
project drawing
"Milwaukee Anemone"
on the roof of the
National Air and Space
Museum

Otto Piene
lithograph poster
33¾" x 25½"
"Centerbeam", D.C.
commissioned by
Smithsonian Resident
Associates

Otto Piene
''Grand Rapids Carousel''
and ''Iowa Star''
Secession, Vienna, Austria
International Biennial
Exhibition of Graphic
and Visual Art
1979
photograph:
Elizabeth Goldring

Otto Piene
"Iowa Star"
Secession, Vienna, Austria
International Biennial
Exhibition of Graphic
and Visual Art
1979
photograph:
Elizabeth Goldring

Otto Piene
"Icarus"
installation in the
Orozco Chapel
Guadalajara, Mexico
1979
photograph:
Elizabeth Goldring